JN087211

英語で学ぶ

Introduction to Accounting in English

会計入門

スチュアート・ブライソン 著

原 俊雄・大森 明 訳

中央経済社

Preface

About this book

Basic accountancy is studied by various types of people for various reasons, such as:-

i University students learning the subject, whether as their major, or as a more minor subject, perhaps an optional one.

ii Trainee accountants and members of accounting departments, who will at least partly use the knowledge acquired in their jobs.

iii Other workers, often at managerial level, who find that a knowledge of the basics of accounting is useful or even expected in their jobs.

As well as people who are native speakers of English, there are also non-native speakers engaged in acquiring a knowledge of accountancy in English. Many of these are people who already understand accountancy to some extent or even a great extent in their own language, but wish to acquire similar abilities in English.

This book aims to provide an introduction to accounting in simple, clear English, suitable for use by both native speakers who have not studied accountancy before, and non-native readers, whether with or without previous accountancy knowledge.

A great many textbooks focus on accountancy as it is practiced in a particular country, and often introduce content mainly or only applicable to that country.

This book does not assume that the reader is mainly interested in or based in a specific country. It attempts to introduce basic and widely accepted ideas which form the basis of accounting, and are applicable in a wide range of countries.

Using this book

Different people will use this book in different ways depending on their existing level of knowledge and whether or not they are native speakers. However, it is perhaps worth emphasizing three things concerning use.

i The words and phrases in the specialist vocabulary of accountancy, usually marked in **bold**, must be thoroughly learned. Non-native speakers should take heart from the fact that many of the words and phrases are not known by native speakers not having accounting knowledge. Everyone, including native speakers, needs to be aware that words do not always mean exactly the same thing in accountancy as they do in everyday life.

ii Where formats and formulas are presented, it is particularly important to learn these. Many accounting problems become quite easy to solve if formats and formulas have been memorized. Often, real understanding comes later with greater familiarity, but while waiting for that to happen, simple memorization is recommended. Key concepts and their meanings should also be memorized and understood.

iii Practicing using examples is particularly important, particularly numerical examples. There is often a large difference of understanding between someone who has attempted several examples and looked at their solutions, and someone who has not. For reasons of space, examples in this book are limited in number. Many more, with solutions, can be found on the author's website (www.stuart-brison.com).

What kind of people are good at accountancy?

Many people probably have the impression that accountants are mathematically gifted. This is not necessarily true. Accountancy depends on the arithmetic learned in elementary school rather than more complex mathematics. Good accountants require other skills in addition to numeracy.

Carefulness and attention to detail are needed in some jobs. The ability to read and understand such content as contracts or tax law is needed in others. Some accountants sit at desks in front of computer screens nearly all day, others spend a great deal of time talking, listening and managing.

There are thus many different types of people, with various skills, personalities and interests, engaged in jobs of greatly varying content, all falling under the general heading of accounting.

How accountancy has developed, and will develop

Up until recently, most accounting was carried out using paper and pens to create records. In recent decades, computers and other technologies such as barcodes have become more and more important. This process of automation will presumably continue in future. In fact, there are predictions that a great many accounting jobs which are more routine will be eliminated by AI (artificial intelligence). Of course, similar predictions have been made about many other fields, ranging from medicine to warfare. It does seem likely there will be great change in the world of accounting too. However, even in future work environments utilizing AI, the basics of accounting as presented in this book will not change, and there will still be a need for skilled humans with a high level understanding of accounting.

March 2020

Stuart Brison

はしがき

本書について

　会計学は，それを主専攻または副専攻として学ぶ学生，そして，アカウンタントや経理部員の研修などで学ばれています。一般社員や経営管理者もまた，日々の業務にとって会計の基礎的な知識が重要であると認識してきています。

　最近では，グローバル化を背景として，日本人のようなノンネイティブも，英語で会計学を学ぶようになってきました。そのような人々は，すでに母国語で会計学を学んでいることも多いですが，英語でも同様の能力を身につけたいと考えているようです。

　本書は，会計を初めて学ぶネイティブと，会計の知識のあるなしを問わずノンネイティブの双方の読者を対象とし，なるべく分かりやすい平易な英語で会計を説明しています。会計の教科書の多くは，ある特定の国での実践を想定し，主としてその特定国でしか通用しない内容となっています。そのため本書は，特定の国の会計に焦点を当てるのではなく，多くの国々の人々に会計の基礎を理解してもらえるよう，基本的で広く受け入れられている会計の考え方を中心に説明しています。

本書の利用方法

　本書の利用に際して，読者には以下の6点をお示しします。
 i ．会計の重要な専門用語等を太字（ゴシック体）で示しましたので，しっかりと理解してください。会計の知識を持たないネイティブの人々も，これらの専門用語の多くは知りませんので，ノンネイティブの読者はどうぞご安心ください。ネイティブも含めた読者全員に知っていただきたいのですが，本書で使用する会計用語の意味は，日々の生活で使用するものとは多くが異なっていますので注意してください。
 ii ．ひな形と公式を理解することが特に重要です。これらを暗記しておけば，多くの

III

会計上の諸問題をとても簡単に解決できるようになります。より深く学ぶことで真の理解に到達するといわれることがありますが，それを待つまでの間，まずは暗記することから始めてください。会計の主要概念と用語の意味なども，暗記して理解しましょう。

iii. 実際に数値例の入った例題を解くことがとても重要です。例題を解いてその解き方を学んだ人と例題を解かなかった人との間では，理解の点で大きな差が生じます。紙幅の関係で，本書では，限られた数の例題しか掲載しておりませんので，筆者（Stuart Brison）のウェブサイト（www.stuart-brison.com）にはこのほかの多くの例題と解答を掲載いたしました。また，YouTube チャンネル「英語で学ぶ会計入門」も開設しています。積極的にアクセスしてください。

iv. 英語を左ページに，その日本語訳を右ページに配置しました。まずは英語ページだけを読み，英語で会計を理解することに努めてください。その上で日本語訳を読むと理解が深まります。日本語訳は逐語訳せずに，読者の理解を促すために要約的な記載にとどめてあります。また，一部は英語ページにはない形で追記しているところもあります。日本語のページには余白も多いので，ぜひ，補足情報等を書き込んで自分なりの一冊を作ってください。

v. 巻末の Question には多くの例題がありますが，読者はすでに英語と日本語で該当部分を理解していると想定しておりますので，こちらには日本語訳を付しておりません。

vi. 本書には索引があります。索引は用語集のように利用することができますので，ぜひ活用してください。

どのような人が会計に向いているか？

　一般に，アカウンタントは数学に長けた人であるという印象があると思います。しかしこれは必ずしも正しいとはいえません。会計では，高度な数学ではなく，小学校で習った四則演算を多用しますが，そのほかに要求されるスキルもあります。

　アカウンタントとしての業務では，細部への思慮深さと注意深さが求められるものもあります。他の業務でも，契約，税法そして会計基準などの内容を解釈し理解する能力が求められることもあります。ほぼ毎日，パソコン画面の前で仕事をするアカウンタントもおりますが，多くの時間をクライアントとの会話，意見の聴取，そして組織の管理に費やすアカウンタントもいます。

　このように，能力，パーソナリティ，関心も異なる人々が，全く違うレベルの仕事をしていても，それらはすべて会計にかかわってくるのです。

会計業務は今後発展するであろうか

　最近まで，紙とペンを使って記録を行うという会計業務が大半でした。しかし，こ
こ数十年で，コンピュータ技術や情報技術が進展してきました。こうした自動化のプ
ロセスは今後も進展していくでしょう。実際，多くの会計業務のうち特に日常業務は，
AI（人工知能）に取って代わられるであろうという予測もあります。もちろん，こう
した予測は，医療から戦争まで多様な分野でも指摘されていることです。会計の世界
においても大きな変革の波が押し寄せているといえるでしょう。しかし，たとえ将来
においてAIを活用する時代が到来しようとも，本書で説明している会計の基礎は変
わりません。スキルを持った有能な人材には，依然として，会計に対する高度な理解
が求められることでしょう。

　2020年3月

スチュアート・ブライソン

原　俊雄

大森　明

Contents

Chapter 7   Double entry bookkeeping part 1   74

Chapter 8   Double entry bookkeeping part 2   94

Chapter 12　Management accounting part 1　　180

Chapter 13　Management accounting part 2　　196

Introduction to Accounting

in English

Chapter **1** Introduction

1.1 Spelling, phrases and currencies

It has been decided that where an alternative spelling exists, the American English spelling will be used. Where alternative phrases exist, in some cases both will be used in the text to increase readers' familiarity with them.

Normally dollars ($) will be used in numerical examples as the currency in this book. Cents will not be used. So examples will use $20 or $800, not $20.19 or $800.58. Note, however that in reality basic accounting work is carried out exactly, including any sub-units that may exist in the currency in question.

1.2 What is accounting?

Accounting **measures, records** and **provides financial information** about an **economic entity** to **users.**

Measuring in accounting has the purpose of deciding a monetary value for some economic activity or situation.

Recording means creating accounting records. This is normally done using a method called **double-entry bookkeeping.**

An **entity** means an organization or body. This includes businesses, whether corporations or those owned directly by individuals.

It has been decided to use **corporations** or **companies** throughout the book to illustrate the use of accounting in businesses, rather than **sole proprietorships** or **partnerships.** However, both of these, as well as other organizations such as governments and **non-profit organizations** (NPOs), also use most of the same basic accounting concepts as corporations.

1.3 Users of accounting information

Users of corporate accounting information can be divided into various categories. The most important examples are:

i **Directors, managers** and other **staff** of a corporation. These are **internal users** of the information.

ii **Shareholders** and potential **future shareholders** of the shares of a corporation. The financial information they receive may affect their decisions to buy, sell or continue to own shares. This category would also include people who give investment advice relating to

第 1 章　はじめに

1.1　スペリング，フレーズ，通貨

　他のスペリングがある場合にはアメリカ英語のスペリングを使い，他のフレーズがある場合には，読者の親近感を高めるために，両方を使っています。

　本書では通貨としてドル（$）を数値例で使い，セントは使っていません。設例では，$20.19や$800.58ではなく$20や$800を使いますが，実際には該当する通貨のサブユニットを含めて，基本的な会計処理が行われます。

1.2　会計とはなにか？

　情報利用者に，経済主体の財務情報を測定し，記録し，提供

測定：経済活動や状況について貨幣価値を決定
記録：会計記録の作成。通常，複式簿記とよばれる手法を採用
経済主体：組織や団体，法人企業と個人企業の両方の企業を含む

　本書では株式会社を題材に企業会計を説明するが，個人企業，政府，非営利組織も同様の基礎的な会計上の諸概念を利用している。

1.3　会計情報の利用者

ⅰ）内部利用者：取締役，部長，その他の従業員

　外部利用者：
ⅱ）株主および潜在的な将来の株主，株式の投資アドバイザー
　　株式の取得・売却・保持の意思決定に影響

shares.

iii **Creditors** and potential **future creditors** of a corporation. Creditors are those who are owed something, usually money. A bank, for example, would normally examine a corporation's financial information before making a decision to lend money.

iv **Government bodies**. The most common example is the tax authorities, but depending on the country and business sector, other regulators may also require financial information.

Categories ii, iii and iv are examples of **external** users of accounting information.

1.4 Accounting work and fields of accounting

People who do accounting work are called **accountants**. They may work inside an organization as one of the **accounting staff**, or outside for an independent **accounting firm**. The recording of financial transactions at the basic level is known as **bookkeeping**, and **double-entry bookkeeping** is the system used to do this. A person doing work at this more basic level is called a **bookkeeper**.

Accounting can be divided into several fields such as financial accounting, management accounting, auditing, and tax accounting.

Financial accounting focuses on the reporting of an organization's financial information, including the preparation of financial statements, to external users of the information. **Financial statements** contain summarized reports and related information, in specified formats and prepared in accordance with certain rules.

Management accounting focuses on the measurement, analysis and reporting of information for internal use by management, for use in evaluating performance, setting targets and making decisions for the future.

Auditing is an independent examination of the accounting and related records of an entity. The financial statements of larger entities are usually audited by accounting firms, and are prepared in accordance with **generally accepted accounting principles**, often abbreviated to **GAAP**. These generally accepted accounting principles differ from country to country. However, currently, many countries already use, or have plans to adopt, allow or at least move closer to the International Financial Reporting Standards (IFRS), in order to produce financial information which is more standardized and makes comparisons more meaningful.

Tax accounting, as the name implies, is the production of **tax returns** and related accounting information to comply with the tax regulations of a country or smaller region.

ⅲ）**債権者**および潜在的な**将来の債権者**
　銀行は融資決定前に会社の財務諸表を調査
ⅳ）**行政機関**
　課税庁，国や業界によっては**規制機関**が財務情報を要求

1.4　会計業務と会計の領域

　会計担当者は，組織内で**会計スタッフ**として，または外部の独立した**会計事務所**で働いている。財務取引を基礎レベルで記録することを**簿記**といい，通常，**複式簿記**というシステムが利用されている。より基礎レベルの担当者を**記帳係**という。

会計の領域

財務会計：**財務諸表**の作成を含む外部の利用者に対する財務情報の報告を対象
　　　　　┗→所定のルールに従って作成される要約報告書および関連情報
管理会計：経営管理者の**内部利用目的**の情報に関する測定・分析・報告を対象
　　　　　┗→業績評価，将来の目標設定・意思決定
監査：経済主体の会計および関連記録の独立した立場からの調査
　財務諸表は，監査法人によって監査され，**一般に認められた会計原則**（GAAP）に従って作成される。GAAPは国ごとに異なっているが，比較できるようにするため，多くの国が**国際財務報告基準**（IFRS）をすでに採用，採用予定であり，国際的な標準化が進んでいる。
税務会計：**納税申告書**および関連する会計情報の作成を対象

1.5 The structure of this book

Overall, the book is divided into four main sections.

Section 1 Financial statements (Chapter 2~6). This section will introduce the definitions of the **elements of accounting**. It will look at the two most important financial statements, the **balance sheet** and the **profit and loss account** (also known as the **income statement**), considering what they mean and contain. The relationship between successive balance sheets and profits is also shown. Important concepts used in accounting are explained. Some specific and important topics – gross profit calculation, inventory valuation, fixed assets, depreciation and amortization – are discussed in more detail.

Section 2 Double-entry bookkeeping (Chapter 7~10). This section begins with a consideration of what economic activities form part of accounting records. It then continues with a detailed study of double-entry bookkeeping, the method used to create basic accounting records. The section also looks at the meaning and use of a trial balance, and the overall structure of a set of accounting records. Two methods of showing accounting data, **journals** and **T-accounts**, are learned.

Section 3 Analyzing financial statements (Chapter 11). This section concentrates on an important tool to analyze financial statements, ratio analysis. Various different ratios, their calculation and their meaning are discussed.

Section 4 Management accounting (Chapter 12~13). The previous three sections concentrate on accounting for events in the past. Management accounting is used to make decisions for the future, requiring a different way of thinking, which is discussed in this section. A key equation is the basic profit equation, which considers the relationship between quantities, price, variable costs, fixed costs and profits. The equation's meaning and use are studied.

1.6 Company terminology and background

It will be helpful to understand what certain words mean and explain about them in some more detail.

Company or **corporation**: Many words are used in everyday English to describe an organization which carries out economic activities. Examples are firm, enterprise, business, company and corporation. People often use these words inaccurately.

The last two – company and corporation – have specific legal meanings. In this book the reader should assume this means as follows:

a The business has been incorporated. This means that certain legal procedures have been carried out creating a legal entity which is separate in law from the person(s) setting it up.

1.5 本書の構成

セクション1 財務諸表（第2〜6章）

　会計の構成要素の定義を概説する。特に**貸借対照表**および**損益計算書**の意味と内容，**貸借対照表**と**損益計算書**の関係，会計上の重要な概念，そして重要な論点－売上総利益の計算，棚卸資産の評価，固定資産の減価償却および償却－について説明する。

セクション2 複式簿記（第7〜10章）

　どのような経済活動が会計記録の対象となるのかから始め，会計記録の作成に用いられている複式簿記という手法について学ぶ。試算表の意味と活用方法，会計記録の全体的な仕組みを見る。**仕訳**と**T勘定**という会計データを示す二つの手法を学習する。

セクション3 財務諸表分析（第11章）

　財務諸表を分析するための重要なツールである比率分析に注目する。さまざまな比率の計算方法と意味を説明する。

セクション4 管理会計（第12〜13章）

　セクション3までは過去の事象に関する会計が中心となる。管理会計は将来の意思決定のために利用される。このセクションでは，物量，価格，変動費，固定費と利益の関係を検討できる損益分岐点分析について学ぶ。

1.6 会社の用語と背景

　経済活動を営む組織の表現には，ファーム，エンタープライズ，ビジネス，カンパニー，コーポレーションがあり，厳密に区別して使われてはいない。

カンパニーとコーポレーション

a）ビジネスが法人化されている。会社を設立した人から法的に独立した法的実体を作るために，法的手続きがとられたことを意味する。

b To raise money for its activities, the company issues shares for sale. The payment received for shares provides funds for the business.

Shareholder: The owners of the shares are called the shareholders, and they are the owners of the company. At least once a year, companies will normally hold a **shareholders' meeting**, at which the financial statements and other matters will be examined, discussed and decided upon. Owning the shares of a company normally gives voting rights at shareholders' meetings in proportion to the number of shares owned.

Director: The directors of a company are members of the **board of directors**, which controls and runs the business at the highest level. The position of director is legally different to that of an ordinary employee, and is a position with greater legal responsibility and powers. Directors are appointed or removed from office by the shareholders' vote.

As mentioned in section 1.3 above, despite being the owners, the shareholders of a company are usually considered to be **external** users of accounting information. This is because most shareholders play little or no part in the running of the company, other than (perhaps) voting at shareholders' meetings. Thus, shareholders do not have access to accounting information in the same way directors and staff do.

However, in smaller and/or family-owned companies, the directors and the shareholders are often the same people. Often a very small company only has one director, who is also the biggest, or perhaps the sole, shareholder

The word **stock** is often used in place of share, and can be seen in the phrases stock exchange and stockholder.

b) 活動資金調達のために，株式を発行する。株式の対価として受け取った代金は事業のための資金となる。

株主：株式の所有者で会社の所有者である。通常，企業は少なくとも年に1回**株主総会**を開催し，財務諸表等の審議・議決を行う。株主総会での議決権は所有株式数に比例する。

取締役：**取締役会**のメンバーであり，最上位で事業の管理運営を行っている。取締役の地位は，法律上，一般の従業員とは異なり，より大きな法的責任と権限を有する地位にある。取締役は株主総会の議決によって選任，解任される。

　セクション**1.3**で述べたように，所有者ではあるが，ほとんどの株主が，株主総会での決議以外，会社の運営に関与していないため，会計情報の**外部**利用者と見なされる。

　しかし，小規模企業や同族会社では，取締役と株主が同一人物であることが多く，非常に小さな会社には，取締役が一人だけで，その取締役は最大の，あるいはおそらく唯一の株主でもある。

　証券取引所や株主は英語でそれぞれstock exchange，stockholderといわれるように，stockは株式を意味する。この用語はアメリカでよく使われるが，イギリスではshareと呼ぶのが一般的である。

Chapter 2 The balance sheet

2.1 Annual reports and financial statements

Companies produce annual reports about their business activities, containing financial and other information. Within the annual report the main parts are the **financial statements**, which are summarized reports showing financial information in a standardized way. The two most common and most important financial statements are the **balance sheet** and the **income statement**, also called the **profit and loss account**.

2.2 The elements of accounting

There are five categories called **the elements of accounting**. These are:

1 Assets   2 Liabilities   3 Equity
4 Income   5 Expenses

The first three elements will be considered initially.

2.3 Assets

An **asset** is an economic resource. It is something of value that is capable of being owned or controlled to contribute economically to a business.

Examples: cash, bank accounts, machinery, patents, office equipment, buildings, amounts owing to the business for goods sold on credit.

Definition from International Financial Reporting Standards:
An asset is a present economic resource controlled by the entity as a result of past events.

2.4 Liabilities

Liabilities are economic obligations or payables of the business.

Examples: amounts owing by the business for goods purchased on credit, bank loans to the business, taxes owed to the government, salaries earned but not yet paid to employees.

Definition (slightly altered) from International Financial Reporting Standards:
A liability is a present obligation of the entity to transfer an economic resource as a result of past events.

The outflow of resources is most commonly a payment of money, but not always.

第2章 貸借対照表

2.1 年次報告書（アニュアルレポート）と財務諸表

会社は，事業活動に関する財務およびその他の情報を含む年次報告書を作成する。

年次報告書：**財務諸表**及びその他の情報

→**貸借対照表・損益計算書**

2.2 会計の構成要素

会計上の構成要素は以下の5種類

1　資産　　2　負債　　3　資本（持分）

4　収益　　5　費用

2.3 資産

資産とは経済的資源である。企業が経済的貢献のために，所有ないし支配している何らかの価値あるものである。

例：現金，預金，機械，特許権，備品，建物，売掛金（掛け－後払い－で売り上げた商品についての代金請求額）

国際財務報告基準の定義：

資産とは，過去の事象の結果として企業が支配する現在の経済的資源

2.4 負債

負債とは企業の経済的義務ないし債務である。

例：買掛金（掛けで仕入れた商品についての未払額），借入金，未払税金，未払給与（従業員にまだ支払っていない給与の発生高）

国際財務報告基準の定義：

負債とは，過去の事象の結果として経済的資源を移転する企業の現在の義務

資源の流出は，通常，貨幣の支払いであるが，必ずしもそうとは限らない。

Examples settled by a monetary outflow: repayment of a bank loan, payment of salaries to staff.

Example settled by a non-monetary outflow: if a business has received payment in advance for goods, the obligation is to deliver those goods.

2.5 Equity

Equity is the remaining (or residual) amount belonging to the owners of the business after subtracting liabilities from assets. In other words, it is the excess of total assets over total liabilities. In the case of a company, the owners are the **shareholders**.

Examples: share capital, retained earnings.

This course will only introduce these two types of equity, although others exist. These are the two most important basic ones.

2.6 The accounting equation

These first three elements are linked by the **accounting equation**:

Assets = Liabilities + Equity   or   **Assets - Liabilities = Equity**

2.7 The balance sheet

These three elements are found in the **balance sheet** of a business. A balance sheet is a financial statement showing the **financial position** of a business **at a particular point in time**.

Here is an example of a balance sheet, showing various categories of assets, liabilities and equity, and satisfying the accounting equation.

This balance sheet has been presented horizontally in two columns. Another common presentation is vertically, with assets shown above liabilities and equity.

貨幣が流出する決済：借入金の返済，従業員への給与の支払い
貨幣が流出しない決済：商品代金を前受けしていた場合の当該商品の引き渡し

2.5　資本（持分）

　資本とは，資産から負債を控除した後の企業の所有者に帰属する残余額である。言い換えれば，資産合計の負債超過額であり，株式会社の場合，所有者は**株主**である。

　例：資本金，利益剰余金
　資本には他の項目もあるが，本書ではもっとも基本的な2つをとりあげる。

2.6　会計等式

　貸借対照表の3つの構成要素の連係：**会計等式**

　資産＝負債＋資本　または　資産－負債＝資本

2.7　貸借対照表

　貸借対照表：一定時点の**財政状態**を表示する財務諸表

　表示方法：次ページの横並び（勘定式），縦並び（報告式）

XYZ Incorporated

Balance sheet as of 30 September 2020   **Units: USD**

Assets		Liabilities	
Current assets		**Current liabilities**	
Cash and cash equivalents	42,412	Accounts payable	99,013
Accounts receivable	12,820	Bank loans	86,025
Inventories	96,008	Taxes payable	34,851
Other current assets	546	Other current liabilities	190
Total current assets	151,786	**Total current liabilities**	220,079
Non-current assets		**Non-current liabilities**	
Property, plant & equipment	125,124	Bank loans	18,500
Intangible assets	26,235	**Total non-current liabilities**	18,500
Total non-current assets	151,359		
		Total liabilities	238,579
		Equity	
		Share capital	2,000
		Retained earnings	62,566
		Total equity	64,566
Total assets	303,145	**Total liabilities and equity**	303,145

2.8 Key points about the balance sheet

1 The balance sheet shows the financial position at a certain **point in time,** in this case at the close of business on 30 September 2020.

2 A distinction is made between **current assets** and **non-current assets.**
More complicated definitions exist, but for the purposes of this book, a current asset is one which:
a) exists as cash (including being in a bank account) or
b) will be converted to cash within one year of the balance sheet date or
c) will be used within one year of the balance sheet date.
A non-current asset is any asset not satisfying the definition of current.

株式会社XYZ
2020年 9 月30日の貸借対照表 通貨単位 米ドル

資産		負債	
流動資産		**流動負債**	
現金及び現金同等物	42,412	買掛金	99,013
売掛金	12,820	借入金	86,025
棚卸資産	96,008	未払税金	34,851
その他の流動資産	546	その他の流動負債	190
流動資産合計	151,786	**流動負債合計**	220,079
固定資産		**固定負債**	
有形固定資産	125,124	借入金	18,500
無形固定資産	26,235	**固定負債合計**	18,500
固定資産合計	151,359		
		負債合計	238,579
		資本	
		資本金	2,000
		利益剰余金	62,566
		資本合計	64,566
資産合計	303,145	**負債及び資本合計**	303,145

2.8　貸借対照表の要点

1　**一定時点**の財政状態を表示

2　**流動資産**と**固定資産**に分類
　流動資産（簡便な定義）:
　a) 現金（手許及び銀行口座にある）
　b) 貸借対照表日から一年以内に現金に転換
　c) 貸借対照表日から一年以内に使用
　固定資産:流動資産の定義を満たさない資産

3 There is also a similar distinction made between **current liabilities** and **non-current liabilities**. Current liabilities are those debts or obligations which are due to be settled (usually meaning paid) within one year of the balance sheet date.
A non-current liability is any liability not satisfying the definition of current.

4 The balance sheet and other financial statements are expressed in a certain **reporting currency**, usually the currency of the country the business is located in. Any amounts in other currencies will be **translated** into the reporting currency. The balance sheet example shown above is in dollars. However, large businesses usually create financial statements using thousands or millions of currency units, to make the reports easier to read.

2.9 Explanation of asset categories

Cash: note that in accounting, the word **cash** usually does not only mean coins and banknotes, but also amounts of money in bank accounts. **Cash and cash equivalents,** the phrase used in the balance sheet, is longer but more accurate. Be careful because there are also be times when the word cash is used to mean coins and banknotes only.

Usually, the category cash and cash equivalents is mainly composed of what is held in bank accounts. In many businesses, only relatively small amounts of coins and banknotes are held at any time, and even if many coins and banknotes are received, they are deposited in a bank account frequently, for reasons of security and convenience.

The phrase **cash sale** emphasizes that it is a sale where payment is immediate.

Accounts receivable (ARs): this means where goods or services are provided to a customer, but payment will be received later. In other words, the goods or services were sold **on credit**, not as a cash sale. Normally such amounts would be received within a year, and so accounts receivable are classed as current assets.

Inventories: these are the business's stock of goods for sale. In the case of a wholesaler or retailer, inventories would normally mean goods bought for re-sale. In the case of a manufacturing business, inventories would normally mean completed goods made, goods in the process of being made, or materials to be used in production of goods. Usually items in inventories are expected to be sold within a year, or be used in making products within a year, and so inventories are classed as current assets.

3　**流動負債**と**固定負債**に分類
　流動負債：貸借対照表日から一年以内に決済（通常は支払）しなければならない債
　　　　　　務，義務
　固定負債：流動負債の定義を満たさない負債

4　通貨及び単位
　財務諸表は，一定の**報告通貨**（通常，企業の所在国の通貨）で表示
　外貨による額は報告通貨に**換算**
　大企業は報告書の読みやすさのために通貨単位として千，百万単位で作成

2.9　資産の部の解説

現金：硬貨，紙幣だけでなく銀行口座の預金も意味する。貸借対照表上の**現金及び現
　　　金同等物**という表現がより正確である。
　　　　現金及び現金同等物の区分は，主に銀行に預け入れられているもので構成され，
　　　少額の金銭しか所持せず，多額の金銭を受け取った場合も安全性と利便性のため
　　　直ちに預金に預け入れている。
　　　　現金売上という表現は即時払いの売上であることを強調している。

売掛金：財・サービスを顧客に提供したが，代金の受け取りが後日となっていること
　　　　を意味し，現金売上ではなく，掛け売上ということである。通常，一年以内に
　　　　代金を受け取るので，流動資産に分類される。

棚卸資産：販売のための企業の在庫である。卸売や小売業では販売目的で購入した商
　　　　　品を意味し，製造業では製品（完成品），仕掛品（加工中），原材料を意味する。
　　　　　棚卸資産は一年以内に販売され，製品の製造で一年以内に使用されるので，流
　　　　　動資産に分類される。

Property, plant and equipment: these are assets which are not normally for sale, and are used in the running of the business. Usually, it is intended to use them for more than a year, often for many years, so they are classed as non-current assets.

Property means land and buildings.

Plant means fixtures and machines used in business. **Equipment** also means, among other things, machines, so it may not always be clear, and may depend on the business's own choice, whether a machine is classed as plant or equipment. In general, plant assets are thought of as larger or less mobile than equipment, but in this book, the distinction is not important.

Another common name for property, plant and equipment is **fixed assets**.

Intangible assets: assets can be **tangible** (such as plant, property and equipment) or **intangible**, such as **patents, copyrights, trademarks** and **franchises**. These intangible assets give a business a right to do or control something of value. Again, normally it is intended to use them in the business for more than a year, so they too are classed as **non-current assets**.

2.10 Explanation of liability categories

Accounts payable: these are payments due for goods and services already received but not yet paid for. In other words, for goods and services received on credit. Normally such payments would be made within a year, and so accounts payable are classed as current liabilities.

Examples: Electricity used, office equipment or stationery bought on credit but not yet paid for, inventory purchased but not yet paid for.

Bank loans: these are shown in the balance sheet as both current and non-current liabilities. Often bank loans have monthly repayments stretching over some years, and so there are repayments due to be made within one year of the balance sheet date (and thus classed as current liabilities) and repayments due to be made after that (and thus classed as non-current liabilities). In many balance sheets, this is the only asset or liability split into two parts in this way.

2.11 Equity and an interpretation of what it means

The third section of the balance sheet, equity, represents the amount belonging to the shareholders of the business. This consists of two main items:

i   Share capital - the amounts received or to be received for the sale of shares in a company **at the time the shares were first issued**.

ii Retained earnings - the **accumulated total** of profits and losses **retained within the company since its incorporation**.

有形固定資産：販売目的ではなく事業活動に使用される資産で，一年超の複数年にわ
たって使用予定であるため固定資産に分類される。
Property（土地・建物），Plant（工場・設備），Equipment（工具・器具・備品）
に分類されるが，PlantとEquipmentには明確な区分はなく，企業自身の選択
による。通常，PlantはEquipmentより大きく，可動性がない。PP&Eはfixed
assetsとも呼ばれる。

無形固定資産：特許権，著作権，商標権，フランチャイズ権のように無形の資産で，
企業に価値あることを実行あるいは統制する権利を与えている。一年超の事業
活動で使用予定であるため固定資産に分類される。

2.10　負債の部の解説

未払金：財・サービスの提供を受けたが，代金が未払いであることによる請求額であ
り，掛けで受け取った財・サービスに関するものである。一年以内に支払われ
るので流動負債に分類される。
例：使った電気料金，備品や事務用品の未払高，仕入れた商品の未払高
〔訳注〕わが国では商品や材料の未払金は買掛金という。

借入金：多くの場合，数年にわたって月次返済が続くため，貸借対照表日から一年以
内に返済を迎える流動負債に分類される返済額と，その後期限を迎える固定負
債に分類される返済額がある。

2.11　資本およびその意味の解釈

資本は企業の株主に帰属する額を表示している。
i　資本金－株式の最初の発行時の受領額ないし受領予定額
ii　利益剰余金（留保利益）－会社設立以降，会社内部に留保された損益の累計額。
利益剰余金といっているが，欠損金の場合もある。

The phrase retained earnings will be used in this book, although they could represent retained **losses,** which would mean that since incorporation, the company has in total more retained losses than profits.

Unlike the asset and liability elements, there are various names for this section of the balance sheet. Owners' equity, shareholders' funds and shareholders' equity are three examples, and formerly the word capital was often used. This book will only use the word equity.

From the accounting equation, Assets - Liabilities = Equity, so what the shareholders own is the **excess of assets over liabilities**, also called **net assets**.

One way of thinking of the meaning of the balance sheet is that **in theory** a company could cease its business, convert all non-cash assets into cash at the balance sheet values, repay all its liabilities, and then pay the remaining cash to the shareholders, as it belongs to them. Other than for very simple or special situations, this is **in theory only**.

2.12 Classification in the balance sheet

The classification of an item in the balance sheet depends not only on the nature of the item itself, but on how it is used, and on the company's business activity.

So, for example, computers for sale are included in the inventories of a manufacturer or a retailer of computers. If the same manufacturer or retailer uses the computers in its own offices, they are items of equipment included in fixed assets.

Similarly, although normally land and buildings are property included in property, plant and equipment, in the case of a company which builds houses, if intended for sale, such land and buildings would form part of its inventories.

資本は，所有者持分，株主ファンド，株主資本とも呼ばれるが，かつては資本（capital）と呼ばれていた。本書では資本（equity）を使用する。

　会計等式では，**資産の負債超過額**であるから**純資産**とも呼ばれる。

　理論的には，事業をやめ，現金以外のすべての資産を貸借対照表価額で換金し，すべての負債の返済後の残金は株主に帰属し，株主に支払うことになるが，きわめて単純で特殊な状況にすぎない。

2.12　貸借対照表上の分類

　貸借対照表上の分類は，項目自体の性質だけでなく利用方法，事業活動に基づく。

販売目的のコンピュータ　　　　　　→　棚卸資産
事務用のコンピュータ　　　　　　　→　有形固定資産（備品）
通常の土地，建物　　　　　　　　　→　有形固定資産
建設業者の販売目的の土地，建物　→　棚卸資産

Chapter **3** The income statement

3.1 The income statement, or profit and loss account

The remaining two of the five accounting elements are **income** and **expenses**. They are included in a financial statement called either an **income statement** (US name), or a **profit and loss account** (UK name).

3.2 Income

Revenue is the part of income that a business receives from its normal main business activities. This is usually from selling goods or providing services to customers.

However, depending on the business sector, the main activities could create other kinds of revenue, such as interest income (in the case of banks) or income from **royalties** (in the case of certain music-related businesses), to give just two examples.

A business can also receive items of **other income,** which are outside its main activities, such as interest, foreign exchange gains or profits on disposal of fixed assets.

3.3 Expenses

Expenses can be divided into four types. The word **costs** can also be used.

1 **Cost of sales:** These are expenses directly related to the cost of the sales, such as the cost of manufacturing goods, or the cost of buying goods for re-sale.

2 **Operating costs:** the expenses relating to obtaining revenue, and generally running the business. These expenses are often called overheads. Another phrase is **sales, general and administration expenses** (often abbreviated to **SGA expenses**).

Several typical examples are salaries and wages, rent, advertising, communications, utilities such as gas, water and electricity, office supplies and professional fees paid to lawyers and accountants.

3 **Other costs** which are not connected to the main business, such as interest paid, foreign exchange losses or losses on disposal of fixed assets.

4 **Corporation (or corporate) taxes**, which are taxes on the profits of the company, also sometimes called income taxes, but not to be confused with personal income taxes paid by individuals.

第**3**章 損益計算書

3.1 損益計算書

会計上の残りの構成要素の2つ，**収益**と**費用**が計上される財務諸表

3.2 収益

営業収益：通常の主たる営業活動で受け取った収益
　　　　　顧客への財の販売やサービスの提供によるもの
　　　　　銀行の利息収入や音楽関連事業の**著作権収入**など，主たる活動が他の
　　　　　種類の収益を産み出すこともある。
営業外収益：主たる活動以外で生じた収益
　　　　　受取利息，為替差益，固定資産売却益など

3.3 費用

1　売上原価：売上高の原価に直接関連する費用
　　　　　製品の製造原価，商品の仕入原価
2　営業費：営業収益の獲得，全般的な事業運営に関連する費用，間接費
　　　　　販売費及び一般管理費（販管費）
3　営業外費用：主たる事業と関連のない費用
　　　　　支払利息，為替差損，固定資産売却損など
4　法人税：会社の利益に課される税金，法人所得税とも呼ばれるが，個人所得
　　　　　税と混同しないように。

3.4 Example of an income statement

XYZ Incorporated	Income statement
Period from 1 October 2019 to 30 September 2020	**Units USD**
Sales	482,362
Cost of sales	379,254
Gross profit	103,108
Operating costs	
Salaries and wages	14,123
Advertising	8,166
Travel	5,561
Communications	456
Office supplies	6,709
Rent	14,590
Utilities	2,874
Insurance	1,300
Professional fees	1,588
Depreciation	4,870
Amortization	620
Interest expense	120
Total operating costs	60,977
Operating profit	42,131
Other income	
Interest income	42
Profit on disposal of fixed assets	6
Total other income	48
Other expenses	
Loss on disposal of fixed assets	16
Total other expenses	16
Profit before tax	42,163
Corporation tax	13,291
Profit after tax	28,872

The above is an example of an income statement, or profit and loss account, in a commonly-

3.4 損益計算書の例

XYZ株式会社
損益計算書
期間　2019年10月１日～2020年９月30日　単位：US$

売上高	482,362
売上原価	379,254
売上総利益	103,108
営業費	
給料及び賃金	14,123
広告費	8,166
旅費交通費	5,561
通信費	456
事務用消耗品費	6,709
家賃	14,590
公共料金	2,874
保険料	1,300
支払報酬	1,588
減価償却費	4,870
無形資産償却	620
支払利息	120
営業費合計	60,977
営業利益	42,131
営業外収益	
受取利息	42
固定資産売却益	6
営業外収益合計	48
営業外費用	
固定資産売却損	16
営業外費用合計	16
税引前利益	42,163
法人税	13,291
税引後利益	28,872

上記の例は，損益計算書の標準的なフォーマットである。
貸借対照表：**一定時点**の財務**状況**についての**静止画**
損益計算書：**一定期間**の財務**業績**についての**動画**

used standard format.

It can be seen that the income statement covers a **period in time**, usually one year, unlike the balance sheet introduced in Chapter 2, which is created at a **point in time**.

A balance sheet is thus similar to taking a **still photograph** of a financial **situation**, whereas an income statement is like a **video** recording the financial **performance over a period**.

3.5 Format of the income statement

In the above format, the income statement is split into five sections in order as follows:

1 Revenue information

This gives information about the income generated by the business's main activities (sales) and the direct costs associated with it (cost of sales).

This section of the profit and loss account also shows gross profit, which is the profit on sales after only subtracting direct costs of the products sold.

gross profit = sales – cost of sales

Note that sales is an element of accounting (an item of income), and so is cost of sales (an expense), but gross profit is **the result of a calculation.**

There could sometimes be a gross loss if the sales amount was less than cost of sales. For a normal business, this would usually be a very bad result, as there are still many more costs to be subtracted.

2 Operating costs

These are expenses incurred by the business in the normal course of carrying out and administrating its main business activities. They are also elements of accounting – expenses, of course – and are listed one by one, and again totaled at the end of the list, giving **total operating costs**.

After this comes the calculation of operating profit (or loss) for the period for the entity's main business activities only. This is to enable analysis and interpretation of the results of these main activities without inclusion of items not part of them.

3 Other income and **4 Other expenses**

These two categories show respectively income and expenses not regarded as being part of the main business activities.

3.5 損益計算書の 5 区分

1 営業収益情報

企業の主たる活動で生み出された収益（売上高）及び関連する直接費（売上原価）についての情報。

$$売上総利益＝売上高－売上原価$$

売上高と売上原価は会計の構成要素であるが，売上総利益は**計算結果**であることに注意しなさい。

売上高＜売上原価　→　売上総損失は最悪の結果

2 営業費（販売費及び一般管理費）

主たる営業活動を遂行し，管理する通常の過程において発生した費用。

これらも会計上の構成要素－もちろん費用－であり，項目ごとに列挙され，リストの最後で合計され，**営業費合計**が示される。

$$売上総利益－営業費＝営業利益$$

営業利益で主たる活動の成果の分析と解釈ができる。

3 営業外収益　および 4 営業外費用

この 2 つの区分は，主たる営業活動とは見なされない収益と費用

多くの企業が主要な資産の購入や事業拡大のために，継続的に融資を受けているため，支払利息を通常の事業活動の一部と見なし，営業費に含めることが多い。

Often, interest expense is considered part of a business's normal activities and included in operating costs. This is because many businesses obtain loans as a key and continuing method of providing finance for their activities, for example to allow major asset purchases or other business expansion.

Interest income is more often looked on as resulting from temporary surpluses in bank accounts, and thus not part of main activities.

Profits and losses on fixed asset disposals are shown in these sections, as fixed assets were purchased for long-term use in the business, and not with the intention of a profitable sale. Similarly, any profits or losses on disposal of intangible assets would be included in these parts of the income statement. The amounts included here are the **profits and losses on fixed asset** or **intangible asset disposals**, not any sales proceeds obtained on disposal.

5 Profit (or loss) before and after tax
Profit (or loss) before tax is once more a calculation result, obtained by adding other income to, and subtracting other expenses from the operating profit.

Tax is then subtracted. In most countries there is a tax on corporate profits, which this book refers to as corporate tax or corporation tax, and this is the tax subtracted here. This tax is an element of accounting, an expense.

Finally, profit (or loss) after tax is once more a calculation result, obtained by subtracting corporation tax from the profit (or loss) before tax.

It is necessary to be familiar with this five-step format of the income statement.
1 Sales, cost of sales and gross profit
2 Operating expenses and operating profit
3 Other income
4 Other expenses
5 Profit before tax, corporate tax, profit after tax

受取利息は一時的な遊資から生じたものと見なされ，主たる活動ではない。

販売ではなく，事業での長期使用を目的として取得した固定資産の売却損益，無形資産の売却損益は，売却収入額ではなく，**固定資産売却損益**，**無形資産売却損益**としてこの区分に計上される。

5 税引前及び税引後利益（損失）

営業利益＋営業外収益－営業外費用＝税引前利益
税引前利益－法人税＝税引後利益

5段階損益計算書
1 売上高，売上原価及び売上総利益
2 営業費及び営業利益
3 営業外収益
4 営業外費用
5 税引前利益，法人税，税引後利益

〔**訳注**〕日本では営業外収益，営業外費用から，臨時的に生じた収益・費用を特別利益・特別損失としてさらに区分し，営業利益に営業外収益・費用を加減した利益を経常利益と呼び，経常利益に特別利益・損失を加減して税引前当期純利益が計算される。

3.6 The effect of income and expenses on equity

Suppose George starts business as an accountant on 10 June. He puts $1,000 into a bank account, which is his original equity.

He has a very simple initial balance sheet as follows, which clearly satisfies the accounting equation.

Assets = $1,000 (in the bank account)   Liabilities = $0
                                               Equity – $1,000

For his accounting work, George needs some stationery, such as files, pens and paper. He buys what he needs the next day for $50 cash. So he has now incurred an expense, which can be called office supplies. How has his balance sheet changed?

His only asset, the bank account, now has $1,000 - $50 = $950. Liabilities are unchanged at $0. To satisfy the accounting equation, this means equity has decreased too by $50.

So the new balance sheet at the close of business on 11 June is:

Assets = $950 (in the bank account)   Liabilities = $0
                                             Equity = $ 950

This shows that **an expenses transaction has the effect of decreasing equity.**

The next day George does some accounting work in the morning and the client pays $200 for this work into George's bank account that afternoon, so he now has a bank account balance of $950 + $200 = $1,150.

So the new balance sheet at the close of business on June 12 is:

Assets = $1,150 (in the bank account)   Liabilities = $0
                                               Equity = $1,150

This shows that **an income transaction has the effect of increasing equity**.

On June 13, he then borrows $2,000 from a friend, Mary, and puts that into the bank account too. This is neither an expense nor an income item. It changes the bank balance (an increase of $2,000) and creates a new liability (an increase from $0 to $2,000).
The financial situation, the balance sheet, now is:
Assets = $1,150 + $2,000 = $3,150 (in the bank account)

3.6 収益及び費用の資本への影響

6月10日に$1,000を元入資本として銀行に預け入れ，会計事務所を開業。

会計等式を満たす略式の開業貸借対照表
　資産＝$1,000（当座預金）　　　　負債＝$　　0
　　　　　　　　　　　　　　　　　資本＝$1,000

6月11日，経理業務のための文房具を購入し，当座預金から支払った。
消耗品費という費用が発生した場合，貸借対照表の変化は？

〔訳注〕英米では，銀行預金をcash at（or in）bankといい，手元現金cash in（or on）handとともに，cashという。企業がよく利用している銀行預金の1つである当座預金では，現金を引き出すときに小切手を使い，それを取引先に振り出すことによって，取引先と現金を受払することなく，取引銀行間で現金の受払を安全，確実に行うことができる。

6月11日終了時の貸借対照表
　資産＝$950（当座預金）　　　　負債＝$　　0
　　　　　　　　　　　　　　　　資本＝$950
費用取引には資本を減少させる影響がある。

6月12日，経理業務を行い，顧客から銀行口座に$200の支払いがあり，当座預金の残高は$950＋$200＝$1,150となった。

6月12日終了時の貸借対照表
　資産＝$1,150（当座預金）　　　　負債＝$　　0
　　　　　　　　　　　　　　　　　資本＝$1,150
収益取引には資本を増加させる影響がある。

6月13日，友人から$2,000の借り入れを行い，当座預金に預け入れた。これは費用でも収益でもなく，当座預金残高が$2,000増加し，新たな負債が生じる（$0から$2,000への増加）。
　資産＝$1,150＋$2,000＝$3,150（当座預金）
　負債＝$2,000（返済しなければならない借入金）
　資本＝$1,150，これは前日から変動なし

Liabilities = $2,000 (loan repayable to Mary)

Equity = $1,150, which is unchanged from the day before.

This shows that **a transaction which affects only assets and liabilities does not change equity.**

This makes sense in terms of the accounting equation.

Suppose Assets (X) – Liabilities (Y) = Equity (Z).

If this is true, then if (for example) a 5,000 increase was made to both assets and liabilities, then

$(X + 5,000) - (Y + 5,000) = X + 5,000 - Y - 5,000 = X - Y$

and so the equity is still Z and thus unchanged.

3.7 Key concepts and ideas relating to financial statements and accounting

Accounting period: A set of financial statements is produced for a period starting on a specific date and ending on another specific date. This period is usually a year, ending on the last day of a certain month and called the company's **fiscal year** or **financial year**. A company's fiscal year can end on the last day of any month of the year, but many large companies choose to have fiscal years ending on 30 September, 31 December or 31 March. Often a company's first fiscal period from incorporation is shorter than a year, as incorporation may not happen on exactly the first day in a month, then from the second period the fiscal periods last exactly one year each.

A set of financial statements comprising a balance sheet and an income statement would normally show a balance sheet as of the last day of the financial year, and an income statement covering a one year period ending on the last day of the financial year.

Example: a company has a fiscal year ending on 30 April 2020. Then for that fiscal year it would produce:

a) a balance sheet as of the close of business on 30 April 2020 and

b) an income statement covering the one-year period from the first transaction after the opening of business on 1 May 2019 to the close of business on 30 April 2020.

Where a business has a fiscal year beginning in one calendar year and ending in another, the fiscal year will be referred to using the later year. Also the initials FY will often be used.

Example: A company has a fiscal year starting on 1 October 2020 and ending on 30 September 2021. This is called FY 2021.

資産と負債だけに影響する取引は，資本を変動させない。

会計等式による説明
資産（X）－負債（Y）＝資本（Z）
これが真ならば，資産と負債がともに5,000増加した場合
（X＋5,000）－（Y＋5,000）＝X＋5,000－Y－5,000＝X－Y
→資本はZのまま変動なし

3.7 財務諸表と会計に関連する重要な概念と考え方

会計期間：特定の日に開始し，別の特定の日に終了する一組の財務諸表が作成される期間。通常は1年で，**会計年度（事業年度）** と呼ばれる。9月30日，12月31日，または3月31日を会計年度末とする企業が多い。会社が月初に設立されることは少ないので，設立1年目だけ1年未満となる。

例：2020年4月30日に終了する会計年度を設定している会社の財務諸表
a）2020年4月30日の営業終了時点の貸借対照表
b）2019年5月1日の最初の営業活動から2020年4月30日の営業終了までの損益計算書

　ある暦年で会計年度が開始し，別の暦年で終了する会計年度の企業は，後者の年度を使い，頭文字FYがよく使われる。
例：2020年10月1日に開始し，2021年9月30日に終了する会計年度の企業は，FY2021と呼ばれる。
〔訳注〕日本では開始する暦年を会計年度に使用する。

Historic(al) cost: this means that, in general, items are recorded at the value of the original transaction, and not altered later. So, for example, if a company buys a tonne of coffee for $50, even if the price of coffee goes up to $53 later, the value of the purchase in its accounting records remains at $50. This is a rule with exceptions, however, and revaluations do take place, but this book will not consider such revaluations.

Accruals (or matching) concept: this is an extremely important concept, meaning that income and expense items are matched with the period in which the economic benefit was given or received.

This means that when payment was made or received is **not** the main fact to consider.

So - for example - a sale on credit, where the goods are provided in December but payment by the buyer takes place in January, would be recorded as a sale in December. The cost of sales for the sale would also be recorded in December.

Electricity used in October, with a bill being received in November and payment being made in December, would be a utilities expense of October.

Salaries costs are shown in the income statement in the month the staff worked. Many companies pay staff in the following month, which means that the effect on the income statement (the increase in wages and salaries expense) is in the month the staff worked, which is the month before the staff are actually paid. A liability account in the balance sheet called unpaid salaries, or a similar name, would often be used to show the amount not yet paid.

On the other hand, rent is often paid in advance of the month it is for, so July's rent might be paid, for example, on June 28. In this case, the rent expense would be shown in July, despite the payment being in June.

The phrase **cash accounting** is often used to mean a method whereby accounting is carried out based on when money moved into or out of a business. For certain special cases, such as very small organizations whose transactions are nearly all cash, this may be acceptable, but in general, businesses must use **accrual accounting**, and this will be the only method discussed in this book.

Consistency: one of the goals of financial statements is comparability, meaning that valid

歴史的原価

　最初の取引価額で記録された項目は，その後，変更されないことを意味する。$50で購入したコーヒーの価格が，その後$53に上昇しても，会計記録上，仕入価額の$50に据え置く。再評価される例外もあるが本書ではとりあげない。

発生（または対応）概念：きわめて重要な概念

　収益と費用項目は，経済的便益を提供あるいは受け取った期間と対応させる。
いつ代金の受け払いが行われたかは考慮すべき事実ではない。

・12月に商品を掛けで引き渡し，得意先からの支払いが1月
　→12月に売上と売上原価を記録

・11月に請求書を受け取り，12月の支払いとなる10月に使用した電気料金
　→10月の公共料金（水道光熱費）

・給与は従業員が勤務した月の損益計算書に計上
　翌月払いの給与
　→勤務した月の損益計算書に，賃金及び給与の発生
　　勤務した月末の貸借対照表に，未払給与（負債）を計上

・6月28日に前払いされた7月分の家賃
　→7月に家賃（費用）が計上

　現金主義会計は，いつ企業に入出金するかに基づいて会計処理を行う手法であり，ほとんどの取引が現金で行われる非常に小規模な組織では許容されるが，一般的には**発生主義会計**を採用しなければならず，本書で説明する方法である。

継続性：財務諸表の目的の1つは以前の年度との比較可能性にあるため，できるだけ

conclusions can be drawn from examination of the financial statements and comparing them to previous years. In order to achieve this, the company should be **consistent** where possible, and use the same methods as in previous years. So - for example - if a company has a certain method of valuing its inventories, it should try to avoid changing this method unnecessarily, unless there are real reasons for preferring the new method. An example of a good reason might be **a change in law or accounting standards** requiring a different method. Another reason might be that it is considered **another method will give more accurate numbers**.

Offset: in accounting, normally only items which are genuinely the same or linked can be offset. So, for example, if a company has a bank balance at Bank A of 10 million yen, but also has a bank loan owing 40 million yen, again to bank A, it would normally be shown **not** as a liability (borrowing) of 30 million yen net but as:

an asset of 10 million yen   a liability of 40 million yen

If during its fiscal year, company X paid 400,000 yen for interest on its bank loans, but received 100,000 yen for interest on a bank account, even from the same bank, this would be shown in the income statement as:

interest expense 400,000 yen   interest income 100,000 yen

Cut-off: Company X has a fiscal year end of 30 September. A customer ordered goods on credit on 28 September, the goods left X's warehouse on 30 September, and arrived at the customer's premises on 1 October. Which fiscal year should the sale be recorded in?

There have to be rules for which fiscal year transactions fall into, and these rules have to be reasonable and be applied consistently. The normal rule is that **a sale has taken place when the goods are under the control of the customer**. In the above example, it would probably depend on the contract, so whether the goods are legally under the customer's control when they leave X's warehouse, or whether control only passes on arrival at the customer's premises, or at some other point in time.

Note that the month the customer paid would **not** be the point to consider.

継続性を保ち，前年度と同じ処理法を採用する必要がある。**法規や会計基準の変更，別の処理法のほうが，より正確な数値を提供**することができるといった正当な理由がなければ，処理法の変更は避けなければならない。

相殺：相殺できるのは同一または関連項目だけで，A銀行の預金と借入金の相殺，受取利息と支払利息の相殺はできない。

期間帰属：X社の会計年度は9月30日に終了する。9月28日に得意先から掛けで商品の注文があり，9月30日に倉庫から出荷され，10月1日に得意先の店舗に到着した。どの会計年度に売上を記録すべきか？

どの会計年度に帰属するかに関する規則には合理性が必要で，継続して適用されなければならない。一般的な規則は，**商品が顧客の支配下に入ったときに売上が生じたとする**ものである。上記の例では，商品が倉庫を出た時点で法的に顧客の支配下に入るのか，顧客の敷地に到着した時点で支配が移るのか，あるいはその他の時点か，という契約に依存することになる。

顧客が何月に支払ったかは，考慮する時点ではないということに注意せよ。

Chapter 4   Sales, cost of sales and inventories

4.1 Goods purchased for re-sale

In the case of a retailer or wholesaler, inventories are normally goods purchased from outside the business, to be re-sold. So, for a retailer of electrical and electronic goods, such things as washing machines, mobile phones, computers and cameras would all be inventory items.

4.2 Manufactured goods

In the case of a manufacturer, inventories are made within the company, and are often divided into three categories:

i **Completed goods** which are ready for sale,

ii **Work in progress** (abbreviated to WIP) which represents partially completed goods,

iii **Materials** such as raw materials, parts and so on which will be used to make products.

Because inventory is a balance sheet account, and a balance sheet is the situation at a specific point in time, for example midnight on 31 December, there will generally be some work in progress, partially made products which need further work done on them before they can be sold.

Example: In the case of a manufacturer of automobiles, the inventory may consist of items as follows:

i **Completed goods**: cars ready for sale,

ii **Work in progress**: partly completed cars on factory assembly lines,

iii **Materials:** parts such as tires, seats, windscreens, and car navigation systems, and other materials such as paint, glass and metal.

4.3 Sales and cost of sales

The top lines of an income statement show sales followed by cost of sales giving below them the result:

gross profit = sales – cost of sales

Note that sales is an income element, and cost of sales is an expense element, whereas gross profit is the result of a calculation. Cost of sales is the direct cost of the inventory sold during the period. (The phrase **cost of goods sold** can also be used.)

第**4**章　売上高，売上原価および棚卸資産

4.1　販売目的で購入した商品

　小売業や卸売業の場合：販売のために外部から仕入れた**商品**。例えば，電気・電子製品の小売業者とって，洗濯機，携帯電話，パソコンやカメラなどが該当する。

4.2　製品

　製造業（メーカー）の場合，以下の３つのカテゴリに分けられる：（自動車会社の場合）
- **製品**：販売可能な完成品（例：販売可能な自動車）
- **仕掛品**（WIP）：生産途中で部分的に完成しているもの（例：組立工程で部分的に完成している自動車）
- **材料**：製品の生産に使用される原材料や買入部品（例：タイヤ，シートなどの買入部品や，塗料，金属などの材料）

棚卸資産の表示：
　棚卸資産は貸借対照表の勘定であるので，期末などの特定時点において存在する製品，商品，仕掛品，材料などが貸借対照表で明らかにされる。

4.3　売上高および売上原価

　売上高および売上原価の表示
　損益計算書の冒頭部分において，以下の関係が明らかにされる。

　　売上総利益（計算結果）＝**売上高**（収益）－**売上原価**（費用）

　売上原価は，ある会計期間を通じて販売された棚卸資産（商品や製品）に直接対応する原価である。

In the case of a retailer, inventory is usually mainly the value of goods purchased for re-sale, plus certain other costs such as shipping, and is usually relatively simple to calculate.

In the case of a manufacturer, inventory costs are much more complicated, as they include such things as labor costs of production and factory running costs, as well as raw materials. This book will not consider how manufacturing inventory calculations are performed.

4.4 A formula for cost of sales

Question: Suppose on 1 January 2020 a business has 2,000 shirts in its inventory. During the year 2020 10,000 shirts were purchased for sale. At the close of business on 31 December 2020, 500 shirts remained. How many were sold during the year?

Answer: 2,000 already owned + 10,000 bought for sale – 500 remaining = 11,500 shirts were sold.

As a formula this would be:

number sold = number in opening inventory + number of inventory purchases – number in closing inventory

and this way of thinking is used to give the cost of sales, by substituting the value of the inventory for the number.

cost of sales = value of opening inventory + value of inventory purchases – value of closing inventory

4.5 Valuation of inventory

There is now a formula to calculate cost of sales. But this still leaves the question of how to value the inventory in each of the three cases above. (Opening inventory, bought during the period and closing inventory.)

Unit value means value of one, so one tonne of coffee or one table, for example.

If one product is considered,

value of inventory = quantity × unit value

Inventory is a balance sheet amount. The value of inventory at the opening of business at the beginning of a fiscal period is the same as the value at the end of the previous period, so this will be known from previous period information.

Example: a company has a year end of 31 May. Then the total value of opening inventory on the morning of 1 June 2020 can be obtained from the previous fiscal year's final balance sheet as of 31 May 2020.

小売業者の場合：棚卸資産の価額は，販売目的で仕入れた商品の価格に輸送等の付随費用を加えたものなので，計算するのは比較的容易。

　製造業者の場合：製品生産のための材料費，労務費および経費を含むので，製品原価の計算は複雑になる（本書では製品原価は扱わない）。

4.4　売上原価の計算

例題：2020年1月1日に企業が2,000枚のシャツを棚卸資産（商品）として保有しているとしよう。2020年の1年間で10,000枚のシャツを販売目的で仕入れた。12月31日の決算日において，500枚のシャツが売れ残っている。何枚のシャツがこの1年間に販売されたであろうか？

答え：すでに保有している2,000枚＋販売のために仕入れた10,000枚－売れ残りの500枚＝販売されたシャツは11,500枚

　以上から以下の式が成立する。

販売数量＝期首商品の数量＋当期の商品仕入数量－期末商品の数量

　棚卸資産（商品）の数量を価値（価額）に置き換えることで以下のように売上原価が得られる。

売上原価＝期首商品棚卸高＋当期商品仕入高－期末商品棚卸高

4.5　棚卸資産の価額

　棚卸資産の計算には，**単価（単位価格，原単位）**を用いる方法がある。これは，たとえば，1トンのコーヒーや1台のテーブルなど，一単位当たりの価値を意味する。ある製品を想定した場合，以下のように棚卸資産の価額は単位価格を使って計算できる。

棚卸資産の価額＝商品の数量×単位価格

　当期首の棚卸資産価額は前期末の価額と同じなので，その価額は前期の情報から入手できる。

例：5月31日を期末とする企業の場合，2020年6月1日の期首時点の棚卸資産の価額は，前期末である2020年5月31日の貸借対照表から入手可能である。

Quantity of inventory can also be measured, often simply by physically counting or measuring the amount of inventory. But what unit value is to be placed on the items of inventory if the historic cost of purchases has been changing over the period, and/or is different to the cost used in the opening inventory? This problem and two alternative solutions to it can be seen from the simple example below.

Example: A company whose fiscal year is the calendar year, 1 January to 31 December, has opening inventory of 100 umbrellas valued at $8 each. It buys 200 more umbrellas at $10 each in February and a further 500 umbrellas in July at $12 each. In March it sells 100 umbrellas. In December it sells 400 umbrellas. All the umbrellas are identical. What is the cost of sales? The information can be summarized in the table below.

Inventory quantity	Purchased	Value per unit	inventory value
100	in previous period(s)	8	800
200	February	10	2,000
500	July	12	6,000

Clearly 100 + 200 +500 – 100 – 400 = 300 umbrellas remain. Thus, there is no difficulty in calculating quantity in inventory. But what should the unit value of these 300 umbrellas be? Here are two methods to calculate it.

4.6 First in, first out valuation method

The first in, first out method, often abbreviated to FIFO, assumes that inventory is sold in the same order it was purchased, and so the value of closing inventory is based on what remains of the more recent purchases.

In the case of the example above, this would mean that the 500 umbrellas sold were those in the opening inventory (100), those bought in February (200) and 200 of the 500 bought in July. Thus the 300 remaining were all bought in July, at a price of $12 each, so therefore:

Closing inventory = 300 × $12 = 3,600 and so, using this:

Cost of sales = value of opening inventory + value of inventory purchases

– value of closing inventory

= 800 + (2,000 + 6,000) – 3,600

= 5,200

4.7 Weighted average method

In this method, a weighted average value for the inventory is calculated, and this is used in the closing inventory and cost of sales calculations.

Weighted average value = sum of each (quantity × unit value)

商品の数量は物理的に計測できるが，仕入れる際の商品の単価が時の経過とともに変化し，期首商品に用いられた単価と異なる場合，棚卸資産価額の計算にはどの単価が適用されるべきか？これにはいくつかの方法があるが，**先入先出法**（FIFO）と**総平均法**を説明する。

例：暦年（1月1日～12月31日）を会計年度とする企業では，1本\$8で100本の傘を期首棚卸資産（商品）として保有している。同社は，2月に1本\$10で200本の傘を購入し，7月に\$12でさらに500本の傘を仕入れた。3月には100本の傘を，また，12月には400本の傘を販売した。すべての傘は同一商品である。この場合の売上原価はいくらか？

商品の数量	仕入	単価	棚卸資産価額
100本	前期	\$8/本	\$800
200本	2月	\$10/本	\$2,000
500本	7月	\$12/本	\$6,000

　このとき期末時点での売れ残りの商品（傘）は何本か？

$$100本＋200本＋500本－100本－400本＝300本$$

　このように棚卸資産の数量を計算することは難しくないが，これら300本それぞれの単価はいくらとすべきか？ここでは2種類の計算方法を学ぶ。

4.6　先入先出法（FIFO）

　FIFO：棚卸資産（商品）が仕入れた順に販売されていくと仮定する計算方法。期末棚卸資産価額は，最近仕入れた商品の価額がベースとなる。

　上記例の場合，期末商品棚卸高は，最も新しく仕入れた7月の単価（\$12/本）となる。

　　期末商品棚卸高＝300本×\$12　＝　\$3,600
　　売上原価＝期首商品棚卸高＋当期商品仕入高－期末商品棚卸高
　　　　　　＝　\$800　＋　（\$2,000　＋　\$6,000）－\$3,600
　　　　　　＝　\$5,200

4.7　総平均法

　総平均法：棚卸資産の総平均価格を計算し，期末商品棚卸高と売上原価の計算に適用する方法。

　上記例の場合，総平均価格は，棚卸資産の合計金額を販売可能な棚卸資産の総量で

÷ (total quantity of inventory available for sale)

Here, the total quantity available for sale during the period is the initial 100 plus the additional quantities of 200 and 500 purchased, so 800 umbrellas.

So weighted average value = ((100 × 8) + (200 × 10) + (500 ×12))÷800 = $11

This gives: closing inventory = 300 × $11 = 3,300, and also

Cost of sales = value of opening inventory + value of inventory purchases

　　　　　　　– value of closing inventory

　　　　　　= (100 × 11) + (700 × 11) – (300 × 11)

　　　　　　= 5,500

The same result could have been obtained more simply by considering that 500 umbrellas were sold, valued at an average of $11 each.

　　　　Cost of sales = 500 × $11 = $5,500.

4.8 Two key points to understand about the valuation methods

Note the following two points:

i)　From the FIFO method: Cost of sales + Closing inventory = 5,200 + 3,600 = 8,800

　　From the weighted average method:

　　　　　　Cost of sales + Closing inventory = 5,500 + 3,300 = 8,800

　　This is **not** coincidence. What has been done is to take the value of inventory handled during the year (opening inventory plus purchases, 800 + 2,000 + 6,000 = 8,800) and **allocate** it either to closing inventory or to cost of sales.

ii)　For this financial year, FIFO has given a cost of sales of 5,200, whereas the weighted average method has given 5,500. This would mean that in this case, FIFO would show a higher gross profit figure for this financial year than the weighted average method. The higher profit amount would be 300, because using FIFO, the cost of sales number is 300 lower.

　　However, when the following year's calculations are done, the FIFO method would show an opening inventory value 300 higher than under the weighted average method, so if this opening inventory was sold, the cost of sales number would be 300 higher at some later date under FIFO.

4.9 Frequency of calculating cost of sales

The example in section 4.5 shows a weighted average for **an entire year**. Weighted averages could be calculated similarly each month, for example, and would not give exactly the same

除して求めるため，総平均価格は以下の通りとなる。

総平均価格 = ｛(100本×\$8) + (200本×\$10) + (500本×\$12)｝ ÷ 800本
= \$11

したがって，

期末商品棚卸高 = 300本×\$11 = \$3,300

売上原価 = 期首商品棚卸高 + 当期商品仕入高 − 期末商品棚卸高
= (100本 × \$11) + (700本 × \$11) − (300本 × \$11)
= \$5,500

上記と同様の計算結果は，平均単価\$11で500本の傘が販売されたと単純に考えることで，より容易に得られうる。

売上原価 = 500本×\$11／本 = \$5,500

4.8 棚卸資産の計算方法を理解する2つの観点

ここで上記の2つの方法での計算結果について，以下の関係が成り立つ。

FIFO：売上原価 + 期末商品棚卸高 = \$5,200 + \$3,600 = \$8,800

総平均法：売上原価 + 期末商品棚卸高 = = \$5,500 + \$3,300 = \$8,800

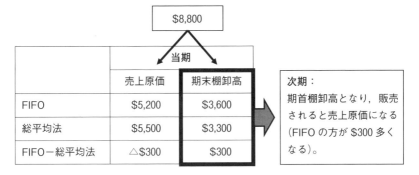

金額が一致することは**偶然ではない**。ここで行われていることは，会計期間を通じて取り扱われた商品の価額（期首商品棚卸高 + 当期商品仕入高 = \$800 + \$2,000 + \$6,000）を，期末商品棚卸高と売上原価に**配分している**のである。

4.9 売上原価の計算の頻度

上記の例で用いた総平均法は**1年間**で計算したものである。1か月や**販売の都度**計算する方法もある。この場合，売上原価や棚卸資産価額は，偶然などの特殊な場合を

result as calculating annually, other than by coincidence or where purchase prices did not change. Some systems even perform a weighted average calculation after **every** sale.

The FIFO method, however, would give the same inventory and cost of sales numbers regardless of how often the calculation was carried out.

4.10 Inventory numbers and reality

This is a good point to emphasize that accounting is a practical subject, and records and numbers produced through accounting should reflect the real world.

Suppose a company's accounting records show that at the close of business on the final day of its fiscal year, it has 60 items of a product, valued at $5 each. This would mean a final inventory of $300. If the company was satisfied that the $5 calculation was correct, it should still confirm that the quantity of 60 is correct. The most certain method would be for a **physical count** of goods to be carried out. Even using advanced electronic systems which in theory calculate inventory amounts correctly, differences are possible.

Question: If the above company found that in fact only 58 items were in its warehouse, what should it do?

Answer: adjust the final inventory value to 58 × $5 = $290

Question: If the above company found that as well as only 58 items in its warehouse, 3 were damaged and now had no value, what should it do?

Answer: adjust the final inventory value to 55 × $5 = $275

Reality takes precedence over theoretical numbers.

Many factors could cause the actual quantity of inventory available for sale to differ from the one per the accounting records. Examples are damaged goods, theft, errors in numbers delivered to or from shops and warehouses, or errors within the accounting records themselves. By reducing the final inventory value in the two examples above, this means the cost of sales was also automatically adjusted higher for the missing and damaged inventory. This can be seen from the formula for cost of goods sold. By decreasing final inventory, the cost of sales number becomes higher, and thus gross profit goes down.

4.11 Checking with reality

Not only for inventory, but in general, an important part of the work of accounting staff within a company is verifying that the accounting numbers and the real world are in agreement, and if necessary, adjusting the accounting records. One vital example of this is checking that bank account balances in the accounting system agree with the information from the bank. If they do not, it is rarely the bank which is wrong! More usually, there is an error or omission in the accounting records.

除き異なることになる。

　これに対してFIFOの場合，計算の頻度にかかわらず，売上原価や棚卸資産価額は同一になる。

4.10　棚卸資産の帳簿有高と実際有高

　会計は実務的な学問なので，会計が生み出す記録と金額は現実を反映すべきである。棚卸資産の帳簿有高（会計記録）と実際有高（現実）は，このことを如実に物語る。

　今，期末の商品として単価$5の商品を60個保有している記録（帳簿有高）があるとする。

例：実際には商品が58個しか倉庫に存在しないときはどうするか？

答え：棚卸資産価額を，58個×$5＝$290に修正する。

例：上記のうち3個が損傷し，価値を喪失している場合はどうするか？

答え：棚卸資産価額を，55個×$5＝$275に修正する。

　以上から，棚卸資産の価額については，計算による理論上の数値を実際の数値に合わせることになる。以上の関係を図示すると以下のように表現できる。

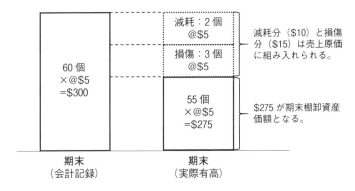

4.11　実際有高との検証

　企業の経理部署の社員の重要な仕事は，会計数値と実際数値が一致するかを検証し，必要に応じて会計記録を修正することにある。このことは棚卸資産だけでなく，一般的な事象についてもいえることである。

Chapter 5 Fixed assets and intangible assets

5.1 Depreciation

For most company expenditure, it is easy to follow the matching principle, and allocate to the correct accounting period, whether the year or the month. For example, if an item of inventory is sold during fiscal year 2020, it will form part of cost of goods sold for that year. Rent paid for the month of June 2020 will be included in the rental expenses for June 2020, regardless of whether the payment was made in advance.

However, it is more complicated for fixed assets – property, plant and equipment. A business normally buys them planning to use them over several financial years. Allocating costs of property, plant and equipment used over more than one fiscal year is called **depreciation**. Depreciation is one of the operating expenses in the income statement format already seen.

Depreciation calculations are done for two reasons:

i) **The income statement reason** – it allocates the costs in a more meaningful way, matching revenue and expenses, over the period the fixed asset is used.

ii) **The balance sheet reason** – it reflects the gradual loss in value of the fixed asset.

5.2 An example of depreciation calculations

Suppose a new business buys a van to be used for deliveries on the first day of its fiscal year. The cost of buying the van is $10,000 and it is thought the van can be used for four years. It will then be disposed of, with a zero disposal value, in other words no sales proceeds. A simple method of allocating the costs of purchasing the van to fiscal years would be to divide $10,000 by four, and include $2,500 each fiscal year for four years as a depreciation expense. At the same time, the value of the van in the balance sheet would be reduced by the same amount each fiscal year, until it reaches zero.

第5章 有形固定資産と無形固定資産

5.1 減価償却

　企業の支出の多くは，費用収益対応の原則に従い，1年または1月といった会計期間に配分される。例えば，2020年度に販売された棚卸資産は，当該期間の売上原価を構成する。2020年6月の賃借料は，それが前払いされたものであっても，2020年6月の賃借料となる。

　しかし，有形固定資産はもっと複雑である。企業は通常，それらを複数の会計年度にわたって使用する。

　減価償却とは，1年を超えて使用する有形固定資産を費用配分する手続であり，減価償却費は，損益計算書（P&L）の営業費用の1つである。

　減価償却費の計算は以下の2つの理由から行われる：

i) **損益計算書上の理由**：有形固定資産が使用される期間を通じて費用と収益が対応するように，より意味ある方法で費用配分する。

ii) **貸借対照表上の理由**：有形固定資産の価額が次第に減少していくことを反映させる。

5.2 減価償却の計算例

例：ある企業が開業し，会計年度の初日に配送用バン（車両）を購入した。車両の取得原価は$10,000であり，4年間にわたって使用する予定である。また残存価額はゼロ，すなわち売却収入はない。

　減価償却の方法：

　もっとも簡単な減価償却費の計算方法は，取得原価の$10,000を使用期間の4年間で除し，毎期$2,500ずつ減価償却費を計上する。車両の価額がゼロになるまで4年間にわたって減価させる。

A partial income statement, and the balance sheet value of the van would be as below:

Fiscal year	Year 1	Year 2	Year 3	Year 4
Gross profit	5,000	4,800	5,100	4,900
Operating costs other than depreciation	2,000	1,990	2,100	1,950
Depreciation of van	2,500	2,500	2,500	2,500
Profit for fiscal year	500	310	500	450
Balance sheet at end of fiscal year				
Equipment - van	7,500	5,000	2,500	0

Another way of showing the van's value decreasing over time is to introduce an amount called **accumulated depreciation**, which is the total depreciation from purchase up to that point in time. This would show the van's reduction in value as:

At end of	Year 1	Year 2	Year 3	Year 4
Initial cost of van	10,000	10,000	10,000	10,000
Accumulated depreciation	2,500	5,000	7,500	10,000
Value of van after depreciation	7,500	5,000	2,500	0

The phrase **net book value** (abbreviated to **NBV**) is used to mean the value of an asset after it has been reduced by depreciation. The term **written-down value** is also used.

So net book value at date D = initial cost of asset

– accumulated depreciation up to date D

5.3 Monthly depreciation calculations

In the initial example of the van it was assumed that it was bought on the first day of the fiscal year. In reality fixed assets are acquired at various times during a fiscal year. In many businesses, depreciation calculations are done to the nearest month, and the month of acquisition of the asset is counted as a full month. So, for example, if a company with a fiscal year end of 31 December purchased an asset on 21 May 2020, the asset would be depreciated

要約P&Lおよび車両の貸借対照表価額は以下の通り。

会計年度	1期	2期	3期	4期
売上総利益	5,000	4,800	5,100	4,900
減価償却費を除く営業費用	2,000	1,990	2,100	1,950
車両の減価償却費	2,500	2,500	2,500	2,500
当該年度の利益	500	310	500	450
期末貸借対照表				
有形固定資産（車両）	7,500	5,000	2,500	0

また，車両の購入から各期末時点までの減価償却費の合計を**減価償却累計額**という。毎期の減価償却費と減価償却累計額の関係は以下の通りである。ここで**未償却残高（正味簿価）**（NBV）という用語は，減価償却によって引き下げられた後の当該有形固定資産の価額を意味する。これは，**評価切下げ後価額**とも呼ばれる。

以下の表から，以下の式の関係が明らかにされる。

ある時点の未償却残高＝資産の取得原価－ある時点までの減価償却累計額

	1期	2期	3期	4期
車両の取得原価（初期投資額）	10,000	10,000	10,000	10,000
減価償却累計額	2,500	5,000	7,500	10,000
未償却残高	7,500	5,000	2,500	0

この関係を図示すると，以下の通りである。

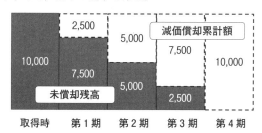

5.3　減価償却の毎月の計算

上記の車両$10,000の例では，当該車両は会計年度の初日に購入したと仮定していたが，実際には有形固定資産は，会計年度中に何度か取得される。この場合の減価償却費の計算は，当該資産を取得した月から行われ，月の途中で取得しても1か月単位で計算される。例えば，12月31日を期末とする企業が，2020年5月21日にある資産を購入した場合，当該資産は会計期間の8か月分の減価償却が行われる。本書の例では，

for 8 months in the financial year 2020. Examples in this book will be calculated on a monthly basis.

5.4 Information required for depreciation calculations

To do depreciation calculations for an asset, four pieces of information are used.

1) The **initial cost**   2) The assumed **useful life** of the asset

3) The assumed **residual value**   4) The **depreciation method** to use

These are considered below one by one.

5.5 Initial cost of a fixed asset

The **initial cost** of a fixed asset includes its purchase price and any additional costs required to **prepare it for initial use**, such as delivery and installation. Normally, for most fixed assets, the purchase price itself is the largest part, or even all of the initial value.

5.6 Useful life

In the example in section 5.2, it was assumed that the van was used for exactly four years. In reality, when a fixed asset is purchased, how long it will be used for in the business is usually not known, simply because the future is uncertain. However, the accounting must be done on a continual basis, and so assumptions and estimates relating to the future must be used.

Useful life means the period over which the asset is expected to contribute to business operations. For example, for a personal computer it might be 3 years, for an office table perhaps 7 years, for an office building owned by a business, it might be 20 years.

In reality, often, a business will divide fixed assets into various classes and assign a useful lifetime to each class. So - for example - all motor vehicles might be depreciated over 4 years, all office electronic equipment over 3 years, all office furniture over 8 years. There is thus often no attempt to judge each asset's lifetime individually in advance.

5.7 Residual value

It is not always assumed that at the end of its useful life, an item has no value. It might be

月割りでの減価償却費を計算している。

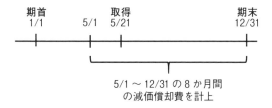

5.4 減価償却費の計算に必要な情報

減価償却費の計算において，以下の4種類の情報が必要。
1) 取得原価（初期投資額）（5.5節）
2) 耐用年数（5.6節）
3) 残存価額（5.7節）
4) 減価償却方法（5.8節）

5.5 有形固定資産の取得原価（初期投資額）

有形固定資産の**取得原価（初期投資額）**は，購入代価に加えて配送や設置といった**使用のために必要な準備**にかかる追加的なコストも含む。購入代価が取得原価の大半，場合によってはすべてを占める。

5.6 耐用年数

5.2節の例では車両はちょうど4年間使用することを想定したが，実際には，将来が不確実なので，その固定資産をどの程度使用するかはわからない。しかし，会計では継続的に帳簿に記録しなければならないので，将来に関するある種の前提や見積もりが必要となる。

耐用年数は，当該資産が事業活動に貢献すると期待される期間を意味する。通常，企業は有形固定資産をさまざまな種類に分け，各種類ごとに適切な耐用年数を割り当てる（例：パソコン3年間，事務机7年間，自社所有ビル20年間など）。

企業実務では，固定資産をいくつかのクラスに分け，クラスごとに耐用年数を設定する。よって，例えば，すべての自動車は4年間，事務用電子機器は3年間，家具類は8年間にわたって減価償却される。

5.7 残存価額

耐用年数の満了時点で必ずしもすべての価値がゼロになるわけではない。有形固定資産の耐用年数満了時点における処分可能な価値が，残存価額と呼ばれる。**残存価額**（residual value）は，scrap valueやsalvage valueとも呼ばれる。

assumed, for example, that when its use ceases within a business, a motor vehicle or an item of furniture can be sold for 10% of the initial cost. Or it might be assumed that old PCs can be disposed of for $100. Such assumptions would alter the depreciation calculations. The value that it is assumed a fixed asset can be disposed of at the end of its useful life is called its **residual** value. Other phrases sometimes used are **scrap value** or **salvage value**.

Using the $10,000 van example again, suppose it was assumed that it could be used for 4 years, and would have a residual value of $1,000. This means that the cost to the business of the van over the coming 4 years is now assumed to be $9,000, being the original cost of $10,000 minus $1,000 expected to be finally received by selling the van second-hand. Then a year's depreciation using the straight line method would now be 9,000 ÷ 4 = $2,250.

A fixed asset value cannot become negative. When the net book value of an asset reaches zero, no further depreciation expense is added. Also normally when the net book value reaches the initially assumed residual value, no further depreciation expense is added and the asset remains at the residual value, even if it still being used.

5.8 Depreciation methods

There are various possible methods of calculating depreciation. There is the one already seen, called the **straight line method**. The formula for the depreciation calculation using the straight line method is:

(initial cost of asset – residual value) ÷ useful life

Using years in the above formula would give an annual depreciation amount, using months would give a monthly depreciation amount.

One more method is called the **declining balance method**. Each year, the net book value is multiplied by a certain percentage and the result is the annual depreciation amount.
The formula for the depreciation calculation is:

(net book value of asset) × (fixed depreciation percentage)

The net book value for a **new asset** is its acquisition cost as no depreciation has accumulated. Suppose the declining balance method was used in the example of the van above, and the percentage used was 30%.

The calculations are shown in the following table:

減価償却の計算方法については後述するが，ここでは，上記の$10,000の車両の例を用い，当該車両の耐用年数を4年間，残存価額を$1,000と仮定して減価償却費を計算してみる。

当該車両を中古車として売却して最終的に受け取ることができる$1,000（残存価額）を，取得原価の$10,000から差し引いて求められる$9,000は，来る4年間を通じて事業に使用される車両のコストを意味する。後述する定額法を用いて毎年の減価償却費を計算すると，$9,000÷4年＝$2,250/年となる。

有形固定資産価額は決してマイナスにはならない。帳簿価額がゼロに到達したらさらなる減価償却は行われない。また，帳簿価額が当初設定した残存価額に到達した場合も，これ以上の減価償却は行われず，有形固定資産価額は，たとえそれを継続して使用しているとしても残存価額のまま維持される。

5.8 減価償却方法

減価償却の計算にはさまざまな方法がある。

(1) 定額法（直線法）
すでに本章で取り上げた方法であり，計算式は以下の通りである。

$$（取得原価－残存価額）÷耐用年数$$

上記の式の耐用年数に年数を用いれば年間の減価償却費が求められ，月数を用いれば月間の減価償却費が求められる。

定額法の特徴として，前節の車両の例をグラフで示すと以下のようになり，毎期一定の金額が減価償却されていく様子がみられる（毎年$2,250の減価償却費が計上され，その分だけ有形固定資産の帳簿価額が減少していく）。

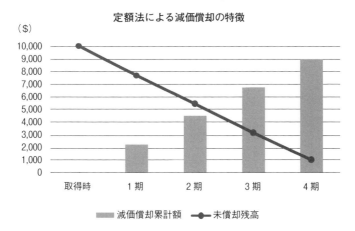

定額法による減価償却の特徴

凡例: 減価償却累計額　未償却残高

Cost of van	10,000
Depreciation (FY1)	3,000
NBV (end of FY1/beginning of FY2)	7,000
Depreciation (FY2)	2,100
NBV (end of FY2/beginning of FY3)	4,900
Depreciation (FY3)	1,470
NBV (end of FY3/beginning of FY4)	3,430
Depreciation (FY4)	1,029
NBV (end of FY4/beginning of FY5)	2,401

The arithmetic is more difficult, but also various differences can be seen compared to the straight-line method.

i The depreciation expense is highest initially, and reduces every year. This could be a more accurate reflection of reality in some cases – say, for a car – because the user benefits more from a new asset than an old one, which needs more repair and maintenance. This may not be true for an office desk, which is perhaps just as useful when five years old as when it was one year old.

ii The asset value, the net book value, will never reach zero. Again, this might be seen as more accurate in some cases as until disposal even an old asset is still giving some benefit to the user.

iii Note **in this example,** the useful lifetime was not used in the calculation.

Note how the reducing balance method is used where the use of an asset is not for a full year.

depreciation charge = (annual percentage × number of months used) ÷ 12

If in the example above, the machine was used only for the last 3 months of the first financial year, the numbers would change as follows.

Cost of van	10,000
Depreciation (FY1) (10,000 × 0.3 × 3 ÷12)	750
NBV (end of FY1/beginning of FY2)	9,250
Depreciation (FY2)	2,775
NBV (end of FY2/beginning of FY3)	6,475
Depreciation (FY3)	1,942
NBV (end of FY3/beginning of FY4)	4,533
Depreciation (FY4)	1,360
NBV (end of FY4/beginning of FY5)	3,173

Sometimes altered versions of the declining balance method are used. One alteration is to

(2) 定率法（declining balance method; reducing balance method）

定率法は，毎期，未償却残高に一定の償却率を乗じ，年間の減価償却費を求める方法である。計算式は以下の通りである。

有形固定資産の未償却残高×償却率

前節で使用した車両の例に定率法を適用し，償却率が30%の場合，以下のグラフに示したように減価償却されていく（減価償却費と未償却残高の金額は，56ページの英文を参照）。

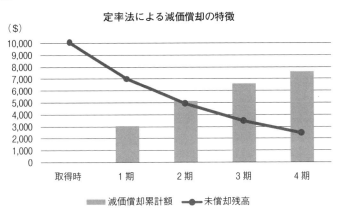

定率法による減価償却の特徴

定率法は，定額法と比べて計算方法は複雑となり，以下の3点で定額法との違いがみられる。

i. 減価償却費は有形固定資産導入初期に多く計上され，年を経るごとに計上額は少なくなっていく。このことは，例えば自動車のようなケースでは，現実をより的確に反映しうる。なぜなら，自動車などの利用者は，維持・修理を必要とする古いものに比べて新しいものの方がより多くの便益を得るからである。

ii. 有形固定資産価額（未償却残高）は決してゼロにならない。さらに，このことは，たとえ古い資産が，それが廃棄されるまで依然として企業に便益を提供し続けているような場合に妥当する。

iii. この例では，耐用年数が減価償却費の計算に使用されていない。

ある有形固定資産を丸1年間使用するわけではない（会計年度途中で取得するなど）場合，定率法においては，以下のように計算される。

減価償却費＝（年間の償却率×使用した月数）÷12か月

例えば，本節で取り上げている車両の例において，会計年度の残り3か月で取得し

assume a residual value which when reached, means that depreciation is no longer calculated and the net book value remains at that residual value. Another altered version is to use an assumed useful lifetime and no longer perform depreciation calculations when the length of time of the useful lifetime has passed. Again, the net book value would remain at the value reached at that point in time.

5.9 Is an item a fixed asset or not?

Suppose a business bought an item with a very small value, such as a stapler for $2. It is quite likely that this could be used in the business for several years. Should it be treated as a fixed asset item of equipment, given an appropriate useful lifetime and depreciated?

The answer is almost definitely no. Businesses often set a monetary limit below which something is not treated as a fixed asset, but as an expense item. So a $2 stapler purchase would cause an increase of $2 to an operating expense, perhaps called **office supplies**, in the fiscal year of its purchase.

In the past personal computers were expensive and so were treated as items of equipment. Now, because of the decline in their prices, often even personal computers are treated as operating expenses when purchased.

However, even if an individual item is below the monetary limit, a large purchase of such items as a set may be treated as fixed assets. So, for example, one chair costing $20 and one desk costing $30 might be treated as office expenses, but the purchase of 100 desks and chairs costing $5,000 might be treated as an addition to fixed assets.

5.10 Land – a special case

Land is normally not depreciated, because it is assumed to have an unlimited useful life. Usually, it remains on the balance sheet at the acquisition value.

5.11 Disposal of a fixed asset

A fixed asset could be disposed of for various reasons, such as because it is no longer used, or is too difficult or expensive to run or repair. In the case of a vehicle, it could be severely damaged in a road accident, and have to be scrapped.

A fixed asset may be disposed of for no income, or it may be sold.

To account for a fixed asset disposal, three things must be done.

a) The final net book value as of the date of disposal is calculated.

b) By comparing this to the proceeds received (if any), the profit or loss on disposal is calculated.

c) The asset is removed from the balance sheet.

た場合，第 1 期の減価償却費は，（$10,000×0.3× 3 か月）÷12か月＝$750と計算される（減価償却費と未償却残高の金額は，56ページの英文を参照）。

5.9　有形固定資産項目か費用項目か？

　企業が，$2のホチキスなど極めて少額のものを購入し，数年間事業に使用するとしよう。このホチキスは，適切な耐用年数にわたって減価償却するよう，有形固定資産として処理されるべきであろうか？

　答えはノーである。企業はたいてい金額の要件を設定しており，その金額を下回る場合，有形固定資産ではなく費用項目として処理する。よって，$2のホチキスの購入は，それを購入した会計年度において，おそらく**事務用消耗品費**という営業費用の発生として記録される。

　しかし，個別項目が金額要件を下回ったとしても，1 つのセットとして大量に購入する場合は有形固定資産として処理されうる。たとえば，1 脚$20の椅子と 1 台$30の机は事務費として扱われうるが，机と椅子を100セットで$5,000の場合は，有形固定資産の増加として処理されうる。

5.10　土地：特殊なケース

　土地は耐用年数が無限なので，通常，減価償却されない。ふつう土地は，取得時の価額で貸借対照表に記載されたままになる。

5.11　有形固定資産の除却

　有形固定資産は，もう使用しないから，または，利用や修理をするのが困難であったり高額であったりするなど，さまざまな理由により**除却**される。車両の場合，交通事故で大破してしまうことがあり，その場合は廃車にしなければならない。有形固定資産は何ら収益を得ることなく除却されることもあるし，また，売却されることもある。

　有形固定資産の除却の処理に関しては，以下の 3 点が必要となる。

a) 除却時点の最終的な帳簿価額が計算される。

b) 上のa)の価額と売却収入を比較し，除却による利益または損失が計算される。

c) 貸借対照表から当該有形固定資産を消去する。

The formula for calculating the profit or loss on disposal is thus:

Profit/(loss) on disposal = proceeds from disposal – NBV at time of disposal

So, to take some simple examples:

i   disposal proceeds 1,500, NBV 1,000 $\Rightarrow$ a profit of 500

ii disposal proceeds 650, NBV 750 $\Rightarrow$ a loss of 100

iii disposal proceeds 50, NBV 0 $\Rightarrow$ a profit of 50

When a fixed asset has an NBV of zero, any money received on disposal is a profit

iv disposal proceeds 0, NBV 100 $\Rightarrow$ a loss of 100

When a fixed asset is disposed of for no income, any NBV remaining is a loss

v NBV 0, disposal proceeds 0 $\Rightarrow$ no profit or loss

The profit or loss on disposal of a fixed asset is the number which goes into the income statement – **not** the proceeds of the sale. Note the position in the income statement, showing that these profits or losses are not part of the normal operations of the business.

5.12 Fixed asset costs after use

After a fixed asset is purchased, it will have both normal running costs, and costs for repairs and maintenance. Such amounts do not affect the fixed asset and depreciation values. They are put in appropriate accounts in the income statement. The cost of the electricity consumed to use a machine would be included in utilities expenses. There is also usually an account called repairs and maintenance included in operating expenses.

5.13 Accounting records for fixed assets

It can be seen from the above explanations that fixed assets usually affect a business's balance sheet and income statement over several fiscal years. Businesses which own more than just a few fixed assets will often keep a separate and detailed record called a **fixed asset register**, showing for each asset such key facts as when it was bought, its initial cost and its depreciation each fiscal year up to date.

In the past a fixed asset register was a separate hand-written book, but now it is usually a computer-based record integrated with the business's accounting software.

Often fixed assets are given serial numbers and physically labelled in some way. This is because a business might buy the same or a very similar fixed asset at different times.

Example: A business buys a personal computer during December 2020, and buys another, exactly the same model, in May 2021. The initial cost could be different, of course. Even if it was the same, if monthly depreciation calculations are done, the computers will always have

有形固定資産の除却益または除却損の計算は以下の式で行われる。

除却益／除却損＝除却による収入－除却時点における未償却残高

簡単な例を用いると，以下の関係が明らかになる。
i) 除却収入 1,500，未償却残高 1,000 ⇒ 500の除却益
ii) 除却収入 650，未償却残高 750 ⇒ 100の除却損
iii) 除却収入 50，未償却残高 0 ⇒ 50の除却益
iv) 除却収入 0，未償却残高 100 ⇒ 100の除却損
v) 未償却残高，除却収入 0 ⇒ 除却損益ゼロ

有形固定資産の除却損益は，損益計算書において売上収益とは異なる部分に記載される数値である。これらの損益は，損益計算書において通常の事業活動の一部とは異なるものとして表示される。

5.12 有形固定資産の使用に伴い発生するコスト

有形固定資産を取得した後，通常の運営コストや維持管理コストが必要となる。これらのコストは，有形固定資産と減価償却費には影響を及ぼさず，損益計算書において適切な勘定科目として記載される。また，機械の作動に必要な電力消費は，光熱費に含まれる。この勘定はまた，営業費用の中の維持管理費と呼ばれる。

5.13 有形固定資産の会計記録

これまで見てきたように，固定資産は複数年度にわたって，貸借対照表と損益計算書に影響を及ぼすので，固定資産に関しては，**固定資産台帳**と呼ばれる，固定資産ごとに独立した詳細な記録を用いて管理することがある。固定資産台帳には，取得年月日，初期投資額および現在までの毎期における減価償却の詳細などが記されている。

かつての固定資産台帳は手書きであったが，今では，企業の経理ソフトウエアと統合された電子的記録となっている。

企業は同一もしくは類似の固定資産を別々の時点で取得することがあるので，各固定資産にはシリアルナンバーが付与され，ラベルで貼りつけられている。

例：企業が2020年12月にPCを購入し，全く同じ機種のPCを2021年5月にも購入したとしよう。取得原価はいずれも異なるが，月次の減価償却費の計算が行われれば，帳簿価額は両PCで異なる。仮に一方のPCが耐用年数内に壊れた場合，該当のPCが分か

different net book values. If one of the computers breaks down during its useful life and has to be scrapped, then depending on which computer it is, the loss on disposal will be different, so such similar assets should be labelled in some way to prevent accounting errors.

5.14 Amortization

Amortization is a concept exactly the same as depreciation, and the calculations are done for the same reasons, but the word amortization is usually used when the asset in question is an intangible one. Amortization too is an expense included in the operating expenses.

Because certain intangible assets such as patents and copyrights only give rights over a certain clearly defined period, in these cases it can at least be seen what the **maximum** useful life could be.

Example 1: A company with a fiscal year end of 31 December buys the rights to a certain patent in January 2021, which it intends to use for making a product until the expiry of the patent rights. The patent costs the company $150,000. The patent rights are for 25 years, starting on 1 January 2006 and continuing until 31 December 2030. What would the annual amortization charge be? What would the NBV be at the end of December 2021? Use the straight line method.

Answer: When the patent began its life is irrelevant. Ten years remain when it was bought, and the rights will be used until they expire so the useful life is 10 years.

Annual amortization = 150,000 ÷ 10 = 15,000
NBV (end of December 2021) = initial cost – one year's amortization
$$= 150,000 - 15,000$$
$$= 135,000$$

Example 2: the same facts as above, except that the company plans to make the product for only five years after acquiring the patent, as it thinks the product will be out of date by then. It also thinks the patent will have no residual value after five years. What would change, if anything?

Answer: although the rights associated with the patent are the same, from the company's point of view it will probably only be used to generate profits for five years. Thus, the useful life is only five years and so the matching of amortization costs to periods would also only be for five years.

るようにしなければ会計記録に誤りが生ずるため，両PCにラベルを張るなどして識別する必要がある。

5.14　償却

　償却は減価償却と全く同じ概念であり，同じ理由で計算されるが，この用語は，通常，無形固定資産に使用される。償却費もまた，減価償却費と同様に営業費用に含められる。

　特許権や著作権といった無形固定資産は，明確に規定された期間に対してのみ有効なので，これらの権利については，少なくとも最大の有効期間を耐用年数として把握できる。

例1：12月31日決算の会社が，2021年1月にある特許に対する権利を購入し，当該特許権が失効するまで製品の生産にこの特許を使用すると想定する。この企業の特許権使用料は\$150,000である。特許権は2006年1月1日から2030年12月31日までの25年間有効である。毎年の特許権償却費はいくらか？2021年12月末現在の未償却残高はいくらか？定額法を用いて計算する。

答え：特許権の開始時期は関係ない。それを取得してから有効期間が10年間残っており，特許権は失効するまで使用されるのであるから，有効期間（耐用年数）は10年間である。

　　　毎年の償却費＝\$150,000÷10年間＝\$15,000／年
　　　未償却残高（12月末日）＝取得原価−1年間の償却費
　　　　　　　　　　　　　　＝\$150,000−\$15,000
　　　　　　　　　　　　　　＝\$135,000

例2：上記の例1と同様だが，企業が5年目以降には当該特許権を使用して生産する製品が時代遅れになると想定し，当該特許権を取得から5年間だけ製品の生産に使用すると考える。5年後には残存価額はゼロである。この場合何が変わるであろうか？

答え：当該特許に関連する権利には変化はないが，企業の観点で5年間だけ利益創出に寄与するとみられる。よって，有効期間（耐用年数）は5年間だけであり，収益と対応される償却費を計算する期間も5年間となる。

Annual amortization = 150,000 ÷ 5 = 30,000

NBV (end of December 2021) = initial cost – one year's amortization

$$= 150,000 - 30,000$$

$$= 120,000$$

Thus, from this example it can be seen that the useful life of an intangible asset such as a patent is not always clear from the period of time the rights last for.

5.15 Accounting uses predictions

Financial accounting is based on events which have already happened. So many numbers used are exact, as final amounts have been paid and received.

However, it can be seen from the ideas relating to depreciation and amortization that attempts to predict the future are also involved because of the concepts of useful life and of residual value. So accounting, rather than only using exact numbers based in the past, can be seen to also use **predictions** based on **experience** and **probability**. An asset used for exactly the number of years of its useful lifetime is an exception! Also, other than where the disposal proceeds are zero, assets are rarely disposed of for exactly the residual value used in their depreciation calculations.

毎年の償却費＝$150,000 ÷ 5 年＝$30,000／年

未償却残高（12月末日）＝取得原価（初期投資額）－ 1 年間の償却費

$$= \$150,000 - \$30,000$$
$$= \$120,000$$

したがって，この例からは，特許権などの無形固定資産の耐用年数（有効期間）は，その特許が権利を保持し続ける期間にわたって必ずしも明確になっているわけではないことが明らかになるだろう。

5.15　会計は予測を用いる

財務会計はすでに発生した事象にもとづくので，財務会計が使用する多くの数値は正確である。しかし，減価償却費と償却費には将来予測という考え方が含まれているように（耐用年数と残存価額が代表的），会計は，過去の正確な数値だけを用いるのではなく，**経験**と**可能性**に基づく**予測**を用いることもある。ただし，耐用年数と全く同一の年数にわたって使用される資産は例外である！　また，除却収入がゼロの時を除き，資産は，その減価償却の計算に用いられた残存価額と同額になることはめったにない。

Chapter 6 Balance sheets, closing the accounts, profits and losses

6.1 Difference between balance sheet and income statement items

Consider a company whose fiscal year ends on 31 December 2020.

A balance sheet is drawn up showing the situation at the close of the business on the final day of the fiscal year. A profit and loss account is also created, including all business activities in the one year period starting from the first transaction on or after 1 January 2020 and ending at the close of business on 31 December 2020.

So in theory this company's balance sheet would show the situation just as the clock was showing 12 p.m., so exactly at midnight on 31 December 2020. The profit and loss account would show everything which happened from just after midnight on 1 January 2020 to 31 December 2020 at 12 p.m.

The next fiscal year would start a second later, on 1 January, 2021.

There is a key difference between balance sheet elements (assets, liabilities and equity) and income statement elements (income and expenses) when a new fiscal year starts.

The starting point (called the **opening balance**) in the new fiscal year for items in the balance sheet is the final amount (called the **closing balance**) from the previous fiscal year.

So, for example, if there was $12,000 in the bank account on 31 December 2020 at the close of business, there would still be $12,000 when the business started its new fiscal year in the morning of 1 January 2021. Similarly if there was a $4,000 liability, a bank loan, on 31 December 2020 at the close of business, there would still be $4,000 owing for this when the business started its 2021 activities. If there was $2,000 of share capital at the end of FY 2020, there would still be $2,000 of share capital at the beginning of FY 2021.

However, the income statement amounts **re-start from zero** when the new fiscal year begins.

6.2 Permanent accounts and temporary accounts

Balance sheet items – the various assets, liabilities and equity items – are called **permanent accounts**, whereas income statement items – those making up income and expenses – are called **temporary accounts,** due to this re-starting process.

6.3 End of one fiscal period and beginning of the next

The process of checking and completing the accounting entries for a year, so that a set of financial statements can be prepared is called **closing the accounts**.

第6章　貸借対照表，決算手続，損益

6.1　貸借対照表項目と損益計算書項目の違い

　今，2020年12月31日決算の企業を想定する。2020年度は，2020年1月1日午前0時から始まり，同年12月31日午後12時までを会計期間とする。この場合，貸借対照表は，2020年12月31日午後12時時点の企業の状況を示し，損益計算書は，2020年1月1日午前0時から同年12月31日午後12時までに生じたすべての事項を示している。

　次の2021年度は，2021年1月1日午前0時を1秒過ぎたところから始まる。

　新たな会計年度における貸借対照表項目（資産，負債および資本）の開始時点（**期首残高**）は，前期の最終的な時点（**期末残高**）と同じである。

　以上の関係は，以下のように図示することができる。

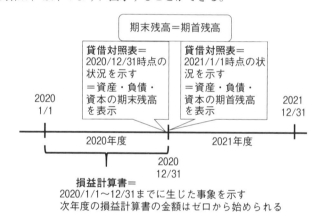

6.2　実在勘定と名目勘定

　資産，負債および資本といった貸借対照表項目は，前期における期末残高が当期（新たな会計年度）における期首残高となる。こうした性質を有する勘定は，**永久勘定（実在勘定）**と呼ばれる。これに対し，損益計算書を構成する収益と費用の項目は，新たな会計年度が開始するときには，ゼロから再スタートすることになり，**一時的勘定（名目勘定）**と呼ばれる。

6.3　会計期間の期末と次期の期首

　財務諸表を作成するために1年間の会計記録を検証し編集するプロセスを，**帳簿の**

This can be thought of as having the following stages:

1) After checking, making additional entries and corrections as necessary, all bookkeeping work is completed for a fiscal period.
2) An income statement is drawn up, having as its bottom line the profit or loss after tax.
3) This amount is added to (if a profit) or subtracted from (if a loss), the retained earnings amount.
4) The fiscal year has now been completed and a set of financial statements are created.

Accounting records for the next fiscal year then commence with the permanent accounts (balance sheet accounts) at the final level for the previous fiscal year, and the temporary accounts (profit and loss account accounts) re-start from zero.

Example 1: At the end of FY 2020, a company has retained earnings of $30,800. During FY 2021, it has a profit after tax of $1,405. Then its retained earnings at the end of FY 2021 are 30,800 + 1,405 = $32,205.

Example 2: At the end of FY 2020, a company has retained earnings of $11,600. During FY 2021, it has a loss after tax of $2,200. Then its retained earnings at the end of FY 2021 are 11,600 – 2,200 = $9,400.

Example 3: At the end of FY 2020, a company has retained earnings of $3,000. During FY 2021, it has a loss after tax of $6,550. Then its retained earnings become negative and are thus retained losses. At the end of FY 2021 they are 3,000 – 6,550 = –$3,550.

6.4 Deducing profit or loss from two balance sheets

Normally, the profit and loss account would be looked at to know what a business's profit or loss was during a fiscal year. However, the profit or loss for a fiscal year can also be calculated by examining two successive balance sheets. Consider the final balance sheets for two fiscal years for a company, FY1 followed by FY2.

6.5 Calculation from retained earnings

If retained earnings from the FY1 balance sheet were $10,000 and retained earnings from the FY2 balance sheet were $13,000, then it could be deduced that the FY2 result was a $3,000 profit.

Similarly, if retained earnings from the FY1 balance sheet were $8,000 and retained earnings from the FY2 balance sheet were $6,000, then it could be deduced that the FY2 result was a $2,000 loss.

締切という。会計期間の期末と次期の期首の関係は，以下の３つの段階として捉えられる。

1) 検証し，追加的な記帳を行い，必要に応じて修正を行った後，会計年度に対するすべての帳簿記録が完了する。
2) 最下行に税引後損益が表示される損益計算書が作成される。
3) この純損益額は，留保利益勘定（繰越利益剰余金勘定）に加算（利益の場合）または減算（損失の場合）される。
4) 会計年度が終了し，一組の財務諸表が作成される。

　　翌会計年度の会計記録は，前期の最終残高で永久勘定（貸借対照表の勘定）が開始され，一時的勘定（損益計算書の勘定）がゼロで再スタートされる。

例：留保利益と税引後利益/損失の関係（単位：$）

	2020年度末 留保利益	2021年度 税引後利益（△は損失）	2021年度末 留保利益（△は繰越損失）
1	30,800	1,405	32,205
2	11,600	△2,200	9,400
3	3,000	△6,550	△3,550

6.4　２枚の貸借対照表から損益を計算する

　損益計算書はある会計年度における企業の損益を知ることができるが，損益は連続する２期（第１期と第２期）の貸借対照表から計算することもできる。以下，6.5～6.7節で説明する。

6.5　留保利益（繰越利益剰余金）からの損益計算

例１：第１期貸借対照表の留保利益が$10,000，第２期貸借対照表の留保利益が$13,000の場合，第２期の利益は$3,000と計算できる（以下の図を参照）。

6.6 Calculation from equity

A profit for a fiscal year is added to retained earnings, so equity increases by that profit. A loss similarly leads to a decrease in equity. However, equity could increase or decrease for another reason, which is that **share capital has been increased** or (more rarely) decreased.

Suppose a company issued $1,000 of new share capital during FY2.

If total equity in the FY1 balance sheet was $7,000 and total equity in the FY2 balance sheet was $13,000, then the increase in equity over the year is $6,000. However, $1,000 of this equity increase came from the issue of new shares, and is not a profit, so therefore:

profit (FY2) = $6,000 – $1,000 = $5,000.

So the profit or loss for FY2 would be given by the formula:

profit or loss (FY2) = increase/decrease in equity between FY1 and FY2

– Increases in share capital + decreases in share capital

例2：第1期貸借対照表の留保利益が$8,000で，第2期の留保利益が$6,000の場合，第2期の損失は$2,000と計算できる（以下の図を参照）。

6.6 資本（持分）からの計算

　ある会計期間の利益は留保利益に組み入れられるので，その利益額だけ資本が増加する。しかし，資本金などの株主資本の増減によっても資本は変化する。

例：企業が第2期に$1,000で新株を発行したとする。第1期貸借対照表における資本が$7,000で第2期のそれが$13,000の場合，第2期の利益はいくらになるか？

答え：当該会計期間において資本は$6,000増加したが，そのうち，$1,000は新株発行に由来し，利益に由来するわけではない。よって，第2期の利益は以下のように計算される。

$$利益（第2期）＝\$6,000 - \$1,000 = \$5,000$$

　上記の関係は，以下のように図示できる。

6.7 Calculation from net assets

From the accounting equation, Assets – Liabilities = Equity.

Assets – Liabilities is also called **Net Assets**. So for a fiscal year:

increase (or decrease) in net assets = increase (or decrease) in equity

So if the amounts for net assets for FY1 and FY2 are known, the profit or loss for FY2 can be calculated (once more also taking into consideration if share capital has changed.).

Example 1: use the following information to calculate the profit or loss for FY 2020.

end of	assets	liabilities	share capital
FY 2019	150,000	95,000	5,000
FY 2020	180,000	145,000	5,000

Answer 1: There has been no change in share capital, so the profit or loss is calculated from the change in net assets.

Net assets (FY2019) = 150,000 – 95,000 = 55,000

Net assets (FY2020) = 180,000 – 145,000 = 35,000

Net assets have decreased by 20,000, so there has been a loss of 20,000 in FY 2020.

Example 2: use the following information to deduce the profit or loss for FY 2020.

end of	assets	liabilities	share capital
FY 2019	150,000	95,000	20,000
FY 2020	180,000	110,000	30,000

Answer 2: There has been a change in share capital, so this must be adjusted for.

Net assets (FY2019) = 150,000 – 95,000 = 55,000

Net assets (FY2020) = 180,000 – 110,000 = 70,000

Net assets have increased by 15,000, but 10,000 is due to the increase in share capital.

Increase in net assets – increase in share capital = 15,000 – 10,000

= 5,000 profit in FY 2020.

This book considers only two types of changes to equity, those relating to share capital and to retained earnings, but there are others, which would affect the above calculations if they exist. However, for many companies share capital and retained earnings are their only equity items.

6.7　純資産からの損益計算

資産 − 負債 = 資本という会計等式から，資産 − 負債は**純資産**とも呼ばれる。よって，会計期間を通じて以下の等式が成り立つ。

純資産の増加（または減少）＝資本の増加（または減少）

よって，第 1 期と第 2 期の純資産額が判明している場合，第 2 期の損益が自動的に計算できる。

例 1 ：以下の場合の2020年度の損益を計算しなさい。

期末	資産	負債	株主資本
2019年度	150,000	95,000	5,000
2020年度	180,000	145,000	5,000

答え：株主資本が変化していないので，損益は，純資産の変化から求められる。

純資産（2019年度）＝$150,000 − $95,000 = $55,000
純資産（2020年度）＝$180,000 − $145,000 = $35,000

純資産は$20,000減少しているので，2020年度は$20,000の損失が計算される。

例 2 ：以下の場合の2020年度の損益を計算しなさい。

期末	資産	負債	株主資本
2019年度	150,000	95,000	20,000
2020年度	180,000	110,000	30,000

答え：株主資本が変化しているので，以下のように調整しなくてはならない。

純資産（2019年度）＝$150,000 − $95,000 = $55,000
純資産（2020年度）＝$180,000 − $110,000 = $70,000

純資産は$15,000増加しているが，$10,000は資本の増加である。よって，純資産増加 − 株主資本の増加 = $15,000 − $10,000 = 2020年度利益は$5,000となる。

Chapter 7 Double entry bookkeeping part 1

7.1 Accounting records

Accounting records can be divided into two main types.

i the **books of account**, which are records created by bookkeeping activities.

ii **evidence** and **backup** such as invoices, receipts, calculations, contracts, information received from banks and so on. These are a combination of materials produced by third parties and materials produced internally.

7.2 Why accounting records are needed

Accounting records are required for three main reasons.

i **Legal:** most countries have legal requirements for businesses to create and keep accounting records for a certain period of time. The records may be examined, for example by tax inspectors or auditors. In many countries, the accounting records must be retained for several years.

ii **Reporting**: to report the results and financial situation of the business. Summarized data from the accounting records is used to prepare the financial statements, such as the balance sheet and the income statement, as well as reporting for purposes of internal use (management accounting).

iii **Day-to-day running of the business:** The accounting records are also used to examine whether payments need to be made for accounts payable, whether accounts receivable by the company have been received fully and on time, whether there is enough inventory, or money in the bank accounts and many other day-to-day matters.

7.3 Ledgers

In the past, the books of account were made by hand, by people writing in books known as **ledgers**. A ledger would have a separate page (or pages, if one page became full) for each separate kind of asset, liability, equity, income and expense. Each of these pages is called an **account**.

So, for example, all utilities expenses would be included on the page(s) of the utilities account. All entries relating to inventory could be seen on the page(s) of the inventory account.

第7章 複式簿記 その1

7.1 会計記録

2種類の会計記録

i **会計帳簿**：簿記上の記録

ii **証拠**および**控え**：送り状，領収書，計算書，契約書，銀行からの情報など第三者
　　　　　　　　　が作成した資料，社内作成資料

7.2 なぜ会計記録が必要なのか

i **法律**：会計記録の作成・一定期間の保存の規定，税務調査官による税務調査や監
　　　　査人による監査

ii **報告**：企業の業績および財務状況の報告
　　　　会計記録によるデータを貸借対照表・損益計算書の作成，内部利用目的の
　　　　報告（管理会計）に活用

iii **日常の事業運営**：買掛金の支払が必要か，売掛金が期限内に全額回収されたか，
　　　　　　　　　　十分な在庫があるか，当座預金に十分な資金があるかなど

7.3 元帳

　かつては手作業で**元帳**という会計帳簿に記入されていた。

　元帳には資産，負債，資本，収益，費用の種類ごとに個々のページ（余白がなくなっ
た場合は複数ページ）が設けられ，それぞれのページを**勘定**という。

　例えば，光熱費は光熱費勘定のページ，棚卸資産は棚卸資産勘定のページに計上さ
れる。

Normally, a different set of ledgers would be used for each fiscal year.

Nowadays, computer systems are used by almost all businesses to keep books of account, and hand-written records are very rare. However, there is much in common with the record-keeping of the past and the computer systems of today, and often they can be thought of in a similar way. For example, in most systems, there will be a screen, rather than a page, where all entries relating to an account can be seen.

Again, similarly to the days of handwritten ledgers, many systems separate the data for different fiscal years into different files. Also even though it is produced by a computer system, the term ledger or general ledger is still often used to mean the business's main set of accounting records.

Most **input** to accounting systems is done by human beings, for example from computer keyboards, and at least some human input will presumably continue for a long time to come. Also, even in highly automated accounting systems, there is still a need for human control and understanding of the processes.

7.4 Transaction flow

Accounting can be thought of as a process with four stages involving the transactions of an entity.

1) A transaction takes place. For example, an electronics store sells a tablet, and immediate payment is received into a bank account.
2) The value of the transaction is measured, in this case the tablet's sales price of $150.
3) The transaction details are recorded in the accounting system.
4) The transaction forms part of reporting, in other words some kind of summarized information. These reports can range from daily or weekly reports needed for the running of the business, through monthly reports, to annual reports for the entire company, including financial statements like the balance sheets and income statements already studied.

The flow can be represented as:

transaction occurs⇒measure value ⇒ create accounting record⇒ summarize in reports.

通常，会計年度ごとに別冊の元帳を使用する。

　現在，ほとんどの企業では会計帳簿への記入にコンピュータシステムが利用されているが，その目的は手書き時代と変わらず，同様の方法で考えることができる。たとえば，ページではないが画面上ですべての勘定記入を見ることができる。

　手書き元帳時代と同様に，別のファイルに異なる会計年度に関するデータを分割しており，コンピュータ上の主要簿は，今でも元帳や総勘定元帳と呼ばれる。

　会計システムへのコンピュータのキーボードからの人による**入力**は，今後も続くであろう。高度に自動化された会計システムでも，プロセスを人がコントロールし，理解しておく必要がある。

7.4　取引の流れ

　会計は企業の取引に関する4段階のプロセスと考えられる。
1)　取引が発生する。
2)　取引価額を測定する。
3)　取引の詳細が会計システムに記録される。
4)　取引は報告書の一部，ある種の要約情報にまとめられる。報告書には日次，週次，月次の報告書，さらに貸借対照表と損益計算書といった財務諸表を含む会社の年次報告書まで，さまざまなものがある。

取引の流れは次のとおり：
　　取引の発生 ⇒ 価額の測定 ⇒ 会計記録の作成 ⇒ 報告書に集約

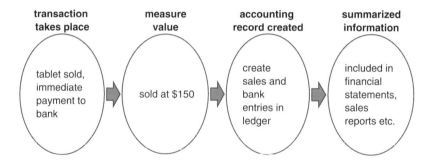

transaction takes place	measure value	accounting record created	summarized information
tablet sold, immediate payment to bank	sold at $150	create sales and bank entries in ledger	included in financial statements, sales reports etc.

7.5 What is a transaction?

An accounting transaction is **anything which changes items belonging to the five elements of accounting**. Some examples of transactions are:

i) **Share capital is issued and payment received for the shares** – which increases share capital (an item of equity) and increases the bank account (an asset).

ii) **Office rent is paid for the current month** – which increases rent (an expense) and decreases the bank account (an asset).

iii) **An item is sold on credit to a customer** - which increases sales (income) and increases accounts receivable (an asset).

iv) **Depreciation of office furniture is calculated and entered into the accounting records** – which increases depreciation (an expense) and decreases the value of equipment (an asset).

v) **Inventory is bought for cash** – which increases inventory (an asset), and decreases the bank account (another asset).

It will be noticed that in each of the above examples, two things changed. However, also note:

a A transaction **does not have to consist of an increase and a decrease**. It could consist of two increases (as in example i) above) or two decreases. (There will also be occasions when more than two items change.)

b A transaction **does not have to involve two different elements**. For example, v) above shows an increase in one asset and a decrease in another asset.

Not every business-related action a company takes is an accounting transaction. For example, merely signing a contract to employ someone is usually not a transaction, as at that stage there is no effect on any of the five elements.

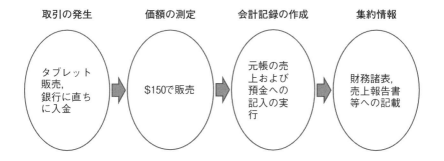

取引の発生	価額の測定	会計記録の作成	集約情報
タブレット販売，銀行に直ちに入金	$150で販売	元帳の売上および預金への記入の実行	財務諸表，売上報告書等への記載

7.5　取引とは何か？

　会計上の取引とは，**会計上の5つの構成要素に属する項目の何らかの変化**である。

ⅰ）**株式を発行し，払込金を受け取る。**

　　資本金（資本）の増加 − 当座預金（資産）の増加

ⅱ）**今月の事務所の家賃を支払う。**

　　家賃（費用）の増加 − 当座預金（資産）の減少

ⅲ）**商品を顧客に掛けで販売する。**

　　売上（収益）の増加 − 売掛金（資産）の増加

ⅳ）**事務用の家具の減価償却費を計算し，記録する。**

　　減価償却費（費用）の増加 − 備品（資産）の減少

ⅴ）**商品を購入し，当座預金から支払う。**

　　商品（資産）の増加 − 当座預金（資産）の減少

　上記の例では2つの事項が変化しているが，ⅰのような2つの増加，2つの減少，2つ以上の変化もあり，また，ⅴのように2つの異なる構成要素を伴う必要はない。

　営業活動のすべてが会計上の取引というわけではない。雇用契約書への署名は，その段階では5つの構成要素に影響せず，取引ではない。

Example: For each of the following transactions, identify which two elements of accounting have changed and whether they have increased or decreased.

a Interest is received in the bank account.

b A patent is bought and paid for from the bank account.

c Inventory for sale is received and paid for immediately from the bank account.

d Inventory for sales is received but will be paid for at some future date.

e A cash sale is made, the proceeds being paid into the bank account.

f Stationery is bought, paid for from the bank account.

g A bank loan is received, paid directly into the bank account.

h A bank loan is repaid.

i An employee works in June, but the salary will be paid in a later month.

Answer:

a Income (interest income) increases, an asset (bank account) increases.

b An asset (intangible asset – patent) increases, another asset (bank account) decreases.

c An asset (inventory) increases, another asset (bank account) decreases.

d An asset (inventory) increases, a liability (accounts payable) increases.

e Income (sales)increases, an asset (bank account) increases.

f An expense (office expenses) increases, an asset (bank account) decreases.

g A liability (bank loan) increases, an asset (bank account) increases.

h A liability (bank loan) decreases, an asset (bank account) decreases.

i An expense (salaries) increases, a liability (unpaid salaries) increases

7.6 Double entry bookkeeping and accounting entries

The method used to record transactions in the ledger is called **double-entry bookkeeping**. The creation of a transaction record is called **making an accounting entry**.

There are two kinds of accounting entries, called **debit** entries and **credit** entries. They are often written as Dr for debit and Cr for credit.

The most important rule about these is:

the value of debits = the value of credits.

This is true for:

i) each individual accounting entry

and so true for:

ii) the total of all accounting entries in the accounting records of a business.

例：以下の取引について，会計上のどの2つの構成要素が増減したのか識別しなさい。

a　利息が当座預金に入金される。

b　特許権を購入し，当座預金から支払う。

c　販売目的の商品を仕入れ，当座預金から支払う。

d　販売目的の商品を仕入れ，代金は後日支払う。

e　現金で販売し，代金が当座預金に入金される。

f　文房具を購入し，当座預金から支払う。

g　銀行ローンを受け取り，当座預金に直接入金される。

h　銀行ローンを返済する。

i　従業員が6月に働いたが，給料は翌月に支払われる。

答え：

a　収益（受取利息）の発生－資産（当座預金）の増加

b　資産（無形資産－特許権）の増加－資産（当座預金）の減少

c　資産（商品）の増加－資産（当座預金）の減少

d　資産（商品）の増加－負債（買掛金）の増加

e　収益（売上）の発生－資産（当座預金）の増加

f　費用（消耗品費）の発生－資産（当座預金）の減少

g　負債（借入金）の増加－資産（当座預金）の増加

h　負債（借入金）の減少－資産（当座預金）の減少

i　費用（給料）の発生－負債（未払給料）の増加

7.6　複式簿記と会計処理

元帳に取引を記録する方法を**複式簿記**という。取引記録の作成を**会計処理**という。

会計処理には，**借方**記入と**貸方**記入という2種類の会計処理がある。

借方：Dr，貸方：Crと表記

〔訳注〕わが国では，借方：（借），貸方：（貸）と表記することが多い。

会計処理についての最も重要なルール：

借方の価額＝貸方の価額

これは以下の2つに該当する：

ⅰ）個々の会計処理

ⅱ）企業の会計記録のすべての会計処理の合計

A debit entry: INCREASES the value of assets, or expenses
DECREASES the value of liabilities, or income, or equity
A credit entry: DECREASES the value of assets, or expenses
INCREASES the value of liabilities, or income, or equity

Another way of presenting these rules would be to use the symbol ↑ to represent an increase and ↓ to represent a decrease, as in the following table.

Financial statement	Element	Debit entry	Credit entry
Balance sheet	Assets	↑	↓
Balance sheet	Liabilities	↓	↑
Balance sheet	Equity	↓	↑
Income statement	Income	↓	↑
Income statement	Expenses	↑	↓

Assets and expenses behave in one way, whereas liabilities, equity and income behave in the opposite way.

7.7 Journals

One way to make or show an accounting entry is called a **journal**.

A complete journal would show a date, the accounts to be debited and credited, the monetary amounts, and a description of the transaction, as shown in this example of inventory bought for $1,000 cash. The monetary amounts in a journal are **always positive**, never zero or negative.

Date: 24 November 2020
Dr   Inventory   1,000
     Cr   Bank account   1,000
50 umbrellas bought from ABC Limited

7.8 More than two entries

The phrase double entry bookkeeping may give the impression that an accounting entry must consist of two entries, but it could consist of three or more, provided the debits and credits total the same amount.

For example, consider one payment of $103 relating to a bank loan, where $100 is a repayment of the bank loan itself, and $3 is an interest amount.

Then the journal could be written either as two journals of two lines each, as below:

借方記入：資産・費用の価額の増加
　　　　　　負債・収益・資本の価額の減少
貸方記入：資産・費用の価額の減少
　　　　　　負債・収益・資本の価額の増加

増加：↑，減少↓で示すと

財務諸表	構成要素	借方記入	貸方記入
貸借対照表	資産	↑	↓
貸借対照表	負債	↓	↑
貸借対照表	資本	↓	↑
損益計算書	収益	↓	↑
損益計算書	費用	↑	↓

資産・費用は同じ方向，負債・資本・収益は逆方向

7.7　仕訳

会計処理を行う，あるいは表示する１つの方法を**仕訳**という。

仕訳には，日付，借方と貸方に記入される勘定科目，金額，取引の摘要が示される。

当座預金$1,000で商品を購入した場合

仕訳の金額欄は**必ず正数**で，負数にはならない。

日付：2020年11月24日
（借）商品　　　　　　　　　　　　　　1,000
　　（貸）当座預金　　　　　　　　　　　　　　1,000
ABC株式会社から50本の傘を仕入れた

7.8　2科目を超える記入

借方合計と貸方合計が同じであれば３つ以上で構成されることもある。

$100の借入金の元本の返済と＄3の利息の支払いで$103を支払った。

```
Dr      Bank loan               100
    Cr  Bank account                      100
Dr      Interest expense         3
    Cr  Bank account                        3
```

Alternatively, it could be written as one journal of three lines, as below:

```
Dr      Bank loan               100
Dr      Interest expense         3
    Cr  Bank account                      103
```

7.9 Use of dates

The date of a journal is normally **when the transaction took place**, not the date that the input of the accounting entry was made.

Sometimes it is not so clear what date should be used, and there may be a choice. A company might make an accounting entry of $1,500 representing depreciation expense on equipment for April. The entry would be:

```
Dr      Depreciation         1,500
    Cr  Equipment                     1,500
```

This should certainly be shown as an April expense, but does not relate to any specific day in the month, so a date of 30 April would be an appropriate choice.

7.10 Journal Examples

Bookkeeping is best learned by examples and practice. Some journals are very common, and so these are examined below as a priority. In order to be brief and focus on the bookkeeping entries required, dates and explanations are omitted from most of these journal examples.

7.11 Bank journals

For many businesses, the most common accounting entries are those relating to bank accounts, either receipts or payments. Money received into a bank account means an increase to an asset, the bank account, and so requires a debit entry. Money paid from a bank account means a decrease in an asset, and so requires a credit entry. But rather than trying to work this out each time, students of bookkeeping should memorize:

Money in (increase) ⇒ debit to bank

Money out (decrease) ⇒ credit to bank

A simple example of a receipt into the bank account is a business making a cash sale for $100. The journal would be:

```
Dr      Bank                 100
    Cr  Sales                         100
```

```
（借）借入金                    100
　（貸）当座預金                         100
（借）支払利息                    3
　（貸）当座預金                          3
```
または，３行に１つの仕訳として記入
```
（借）借入金                    100
（借）支払利息                    3
　（貸）当座預金                         103
```

7.9　日付の使用

　仕訳の日付は**取引発生日**であり，会計処理の入力日ではない。

　日付がはっきりせず，選択できる場合もある。会社は４月中の備品の減価償却費を計上する$1,500の会計処理を行う。
```
（借）減価償却費                 1,500
　（貸）備品                            1,500
```

　これは４月の費用として表示されるが，特定日には関係しないので，４月30日が適切な選択である。

7.10　仕訳例

　簿記は設例と実践で学ぶのが最善である。一般的な仕訳について簡潔に要点を説明するため，仕訳例からは日付と摘要を省略する。

7.11　当座預金の仕訳

　当座預金への入金：資産である当座預金の増加，借方記入

　当座預金からの出金：資産の減少，貸方記入

　入金（増加）⇒当座預金への借方記入

　出金（減少）⇒当座預金への貸方記入

〈当座預金への入金の例〉

　$100の当座預金による売上。
```
（借）当座預金                    100
　（貸）売上                            100
```

If a company is set up, often its first accounting entry will often be the issue of share capital, which is paid into its bank account. If a company received $2,000 for an issue of share capital, then an asset – the bank account – has increased and an equity account – share capital – has also increased. Thus the journal would be:

Dr	Bank	2,000	
Cr	Share capital		2,000

A similar journal would also be used for any future increases in share capital.

A simple example of a payment would be if a company pays $1,000 cash for a factory machine, to be treated as a fixed asset. An asset – a piece of equipment – has increased and another asset – the bank account – has deceased.

Dr	Fixed asset - equipment	1,000	
Cr	Bank		1,000

If a company paid a lawyer $500, the journal would be:

Dr	Professional fees	500	
Cr	Bank		500

This is an example of an expense paid cash, and in general, expenses paid for in cash (so where payment for the goods or services was immediate) would be treated in the same way, by the journal:

Dr	(expense account name)	X	
Cr	Bank		X

The journal for an inventory purchase of $2,000 for cash would be:

Dr	Inventory	2,000	
Cr	Bank		2,000

If money has been received or paid, often the easiest way to write the journal is to work out the bank part first. So first write down the debit or credit to the bank account as appropriate. If it is a two-line journal and the bank account side is a debit, then clearly the other line of the journal must be a credit. Similarly, if the bank account side is a credit, then clearly the other line of the journal must be a debit.

会社設立時の株式の発行による当座預金への払込，将来の増資も同様。

（借）当座預金 2,000
　（貸）資本金 2,000

〈当座預金からの出金の例〉

固定資産として使用する工場の機械について当座預金から$1,000支払う。

（借）固定資産 − 機械装置 1,000
　（貸）当座預金 1,000

弁護士に当座預金から$500支払う。

（借）支払報酬 500
　（貸）当座預金 500

当座預金から諸費用を支払う（財やサービスについて即時払いの場合）。

（借）費用の勘定科目 X
　（貸）当座預金 X

商品$2,000を仕入れ，当座預金から支払う。

（借）商品 2,000
　（貸）当座預金 2,000

　最も簡単な仕訳の方法は，入出金があった場合，まず当座預金勘定を該当する借方か貸方に記入し，相手勘定を別の行に記入する。

7.12 Sales on credit

It is very common for businesses to sell goods or provide services on credit, receiving payment later, and so the pattern of accounting entries relating to this must be learnt well.

Example: On 23 April, a company sells goods on credit to a customer for $80. On 12 May, the customer pays.

One journal showing the sale would be created dated 23 April.

Dr	Accounts receivable	80	
Cr	Sales		80

Another journal showing receipt of the money would be created dated 12 May.

Dr	Bank	80	
Cr	Accounts receivable		80

7.13 Purchases on credit

It is also very common for businesses to receive goods or services on credit, making payment later, and so this pattern of accounting entries must also be learnt well.

Example: A company buys inventory for $150 on 3 April, and pays for it on 12 June.

One journal showing the purchase would be created dated 3 April.

Dr	Inventory	150	
Cr	Accounts payable		150

Another journal showing payment would be created dated 12 June.

Dr	Accounts payable	150	
Cr	Bank		150

The same pattern would be shown for many operating expenses. A company might receive a bill of $35 dated 31 August for electricity used in August, and pay the bill on 29 September. This requires a journal showing the expense and liability dated 31 August.

Dr	Utilities	35	
Cr	Accounts payable		35

Then there is a journal for payment of the liability dated 29 September.

Dr	Accounts payable	35	
Cr	Bank		35

7.12 掛け売り上げ

企業が商品やサービスを掛けで売り上げ，後日支払いを受けることが一般的である。

例：4月23日に商品$80を掛けで売り上げ，5月12日に代金を受け取る。

4月23日
  （借）売掛金   80
    （貸）売上   80

5月12日
  （借）当座預金   80
    （貸）売掛金   80

7.13 掛け仕入れ

企業が商品やサービスを掛けで仕入れ，後日支払うことも一般的である。

例：4月3日に$150で商品を仕入れ，6月12日に代金を支払う。
4月3日
  （借）商品   150
    （貸）買掛金   150

6月12日
  （借）買掛金   150
    （貸）当座預金   150

営業費も同様である。8月31日に8月の電気代$35の請求書を受け取り，9月29日に支払う。
8月31日
  （借）水道光熱費   35
    （貸）未払金   35

9月29日
  （借）未払金   35
    （貸）当座預金   35

7.14 Fixed assets and depreciation

The journal entry for a fixed asset paid for immediately would be as shown above, and a fixed asset bought on credit would have entries like any other account payable.

Depreciation is an expense (so a debit entry increases it), and the effect is to decrease the asset value (a credit entry). Thus, the entry for the depreciation of an office building of $3,000 is:

Dr	Depreciation	3,000	
Cr	Property - building		3,000

7.15 Disposal of fixed assets

Example: A company has three equipment assets and disposes of all three. The information about them is as in the table.

Asset	NBV at time of disposal	Proceeds
A	3,000	3,500
B	1,200	400
C	2,000	0

The journals would be of the following pattern, so if disposal proceeds are not zero, the journal is three lines rather than two.

Dr	Bank – proceeds if any	X	
Cr	NBV to remove asset		Y
Dr or			
Cr	Profit or loss on disposal	(Z)	(Z)

A debit entry records the increase in the bank account, then a credit entry reduces fixed assets by the net book value of the asset disposed of. Finally a credit entry is made for any profit on disposal, or a debit entry is made for a loss on disposal.

The journal for A's disposal would be:

Dr	Bank	3,500	
Cr	Equipment		3,000
Cr	Profit on disposal		500

〔訳注〕日本ではaccount payableを，頻繁に取引する商品や材料の仕入れについての未払高は買掛金，それ以外の資産や諸費用についての未払高は未払金と呼び，両者を区別している。

7.14　固定資産と減価償却

　減価償却費は費用（借方記入），その結果資産の価額が減少（貸方記入）
　オフィスビルの$3,000の減価償却に関する記入
（借）減価償却費　　　　　　　　3,000
　（貸）有形固定資産 – 建物　　　　　　　　　　3,000

7.15　固定資産の処分と減価償却

３つの備品の売却処分

資　　産	処分時の帳簿価額	収　　入
A	3,000	3,500
B	1,200	400
C	2,000	0

（借）当座預金 – 収入がある場合　　　　X
　（貸）除却資産の帳簿価額　　　　　　　　　　Y
（借）または（貸）売却損益　　　　（Z）　　（Z）

　借方記入：当座預金の増加。
　貸方記入：処分した固定資産の正味簿価の減額。
　売却益を貸方記入するか，売却損を借方記入する。

Aの売却処分
　（借）当座預金　　　　　　　　3,500
　　（貸）備品　　　　　　　　　　　3,000
　　（貸）固定資産売却益　　　　　　　500

The journal for B's disposal would be:

Dr	Bank	400	
Cr	Equipment		1,200
Dr	Loss on disposal	800	

Asset C's disposal would only require two lines and is of course a loss.

Dr	Loss on disposal	2,000	
Cr	Equipment		2,000

Bの売却処分
　　（借）当座預金　　　　　　　　400
　　　（貸）備品　　　　　　　　　　　　　　1,200
　　（借）固定資産売却損　　　　　800

Cの売却処分
　　（借）固定資産売却損　　　　2,000
　　　（貸）備品　　　　　　　　　　　　　　2,000

Chapter 8 Double entry bookkeeping part 2

8.1 Wages and salaries

Some companies pay staff in the same month as they work. This would mean that the salaries journal would simply be as follows, for salaries of $4,000:

Dr	Wages and salaries	4,000	
Cr	Bank		4,000

However, many businesses pay staff a month in arrears. This is because, especially when salaries are not fixed, time is needed to perform payroll calculations, and set up payments to workers' bank accounts. So, for example, work may be performed in June but the payments to the workers take place sometime in July.

The matching principle means that as the company has received the economic benefit of the work in June, it should be an expense in June. Suppose wages and salaries relating to June work were $ 2,500. The accounting entry for June, perhaps dated 30 June, would be:

Dr	Wages and salaries	2,500	
Cr	Unpaid wages and salaries		2,500

Unpaid wages and salaries would be a current liability on the balance sheet.

If payment of the wages and salaries took place on July 17, the accounting entry dated that day to record payment and remove the liability would be:

Dr	Unpaid wages and salaries	2,500	
Cr	Bank		2,500

This means that typically many businesses have a liability at the end of each month representing the unpaid wages and salaries, which will be removed the next month when payment takes place, and replaced by another liability (usually for a different amount) for the work done that month.

The entries above for wages and salaries are a simplification, because in fact income taxes payable by the workers, social security and perhaps other amounts would normally also be present in payroll calculations.

第**8**章　複式簿記　その2

8.1　賃金と給料

従業員の勤務した月に給料を支払う。
（借）賃金及び給料　　　　　　　　　4,000
　（貸）当座預金　　　　　　　　　　　　　　4,000

多くの企業では従業員の勤務した翌月に給料を支払う。

勤務した6月にその仕事の経済的便益を受け取っていたので，対応原則により，6月の損益計算書の費用に計上しなければならない。6月の賃金及び給料が$2,500であったとする。
（借）賃金及び給料　　　　　　　　　2,500
　（貸）未払賃金及び給料　　　　　　　　　　2,500

未払賃金及び給料は，貸借対照表の流動負債である。
その支払が7月17日に行われた。
（借）未払賃金及び給料　　　　　　　2,500
　（貸）当座預金　　　　　　　　　　　　　　2,500

多くの企業が毎月末に未払賃金及び給料という負債を計上し，その支払いが行われる翌月に消滅し，その月に行われた業務に対する異なる額の同様の負債に置き換えられる。

上記の仕訳は単純化しており，実務上，従業員が支払うべき所得税，社会保険料等が給与計算に含まれる。

8.2 Bank loans, principal and interest

Suppose on 10 January 2020 a company whose fiscal year is the calendar year obtains a bank loan of $24,000. It is repayable in equal monthly instalments of $500 on the 28th day of each month, being 48 payments over four years, and there is also interest due on the loan of $38 per month.

Normally, the loan would be paid by the lending bank into the company's bank account. This would mean that a company asset, the bank balance, has increased, and so has a liability, a loan which has to be repaid.

The $500 monthly repayment reduces the amount of the loan outstanding. This is called a repayment of **principal**, and reduces the liability in the balance sheet. The $38 payment is classed as an expense in the income statement, interest expense.

8.3 Balance sheet presentation of loans

The $24,000 loan should be split into two amounts in the balance sheet, at the time it is first received on 10 January 2020.

i   A current liability of $6,000 (as $12 \times \$500$ is due to be repaid within one year).

ii A non-current liability of $18,000 (as $36 \times \$500$ is due to be repaid after more than one year).

This would mean that at the end of December 2020, after 12 repayments, there would be a remaining total liability of $18,000. This would again be split into two amounts in the balance sheet.

i   A current liability of $6,000 (as again $12 \times \$ 500$ is due to be repaid within one year).

ii A non-current liability of $12,000 (as $24 \times \$500$ is due to be repaid after more than one year).

Thus, as the loan is repaid, the total liabilities decrease, and the non-current parts of the loan liability become current as they move closer in time.

The situation in the balance sheet and the effect on the income statement from the date of receipt of the loan and for the next three fiscal year ends would be as follows.

	10 Jan 2020	31 Dec 2020	31 Dec 2021	31 Dec 2022
Balance sheet				
Loan – current liability	6,000	6,000	6,000	6,000
Loan – non-current liability	18,000	12,000	6,000	0
Income statement				
Interest expense		456	456	456

8.2 借入金，元本および利息

2020年1月10日，会計年度が暦年の会社が$24,000の借り入れを行った。毎月28日に，$500の均等額の月賦で返済され，4年にわたり48回の支払があり，毎月$38の利息がある。

借入金は通常，融資した銀行が会社の当座預金に振り込む。資産である当座預金が増加し，負債である借入金が増加する。

毎月$500の借入金の残高，元本が減少し，貸借対照表の負債が減少する。$38の支払利息が損益計算書の費用として計上される。

8.3 貸借対照表の表示

$24,000の借入金は，貸借対照表上，2つに分割
i $6,000の流動負債（12×$500は1年以内に支払期日となるので）
ii $18,000の固定負債（36×$500は1年超の支払期日となるので）

借入金の返済により負債合計が減少し，固定負債は期限が近づくにつれて流動化する。

各年度の貸借対照表と損益計算書の状況

	2020.1/10	2020.12/31	2021.12/31	2022.12/31
貸借対照表				
借入金－流動負債	6,000	6,000	6,000	6,000
借入金－固定負債	18,000	12,000	6,000	0
損益計算書				
支払利息		456	456	456

返済の3年目末までに流動負債だけになり，2023年度中に完済される。

As the loan is repaid and time passes, the amounts in non-current liabilities change to become current liabilities, and by the end of three years of repayments, only current liabilities remain, which are all repaid during FY 2023, along with another $456 interest expense.

8.4 Journals relating to loans

The example above will be used to illustrate the journals required.

The first journal, dated 10 January 2020, would show the money being received in the bank account and the current and non-current liabilities being created.

Dr	Bank	24,000	
Cr	Loan – current liability		6,000
Cr	Loan – non-current liability		18,000

For each repayment of principal and payment of interest, there would be a journal on the 28th day of each month.

Dr	Loan – current liability	500	
Cr	Bank		500
Dr	Interest expense	38	
Cr	Bank		38

There would also be the need to transfer amounts from non-current liabilities to current liabilities as the payment dates move closer. The entry could be done once a year, dated 31 December as follows:

Dr	Loan – non-current liability	6,000	
Cr	Loan – current liability		6,000

Alternatively, the same journal could be done monthly, using $500 per month. This is more accurate but also takes more work. There would be twelve journals instead of one.

8.5 Corporate bonds

Another way companies have of borrowing money is by issuing a **corporate bond**. This is a way of borrowing money directly from investors. Normally interest is paid by the issuer of the bond to the owners of the bond, called **bondholders**, although payments are less frequent, normally once or twice a year. Also normally the full amount borrowed is repaid at once, which is called **redeeming the bond**. Bondholders can sell the bond to other investors, so any interest payments and the final **redemption** (repayment) amount are paid to the bondholders at that time.

8.4　借入金に関する仕訳

2020年 1 月10日　当座預金勘定への入金，流動負債と固定負債の発生
（借）当座預金　　　　　　　　　24,000
　（貸）借入金－流動負債　　　　　　　　　6,000
　（貸）借入金－固定負債　　　　　　　　　18,000

毎月28日　元本の返済と利息の支払
（借）借入金－流動負債　　　　　500
　（貸）当座預金　　　　　　　　　　　　500
（借）支払利息　　　　　　　　　38
　（貸）当座預金　　　　　　　　　　　　38

12月31日　固定負債から流動負債への振り替え
（借）借入金－固定負債　　　　　6,000
　（貸）借入金－流動負債　　　　　　　　6,000

あるいは，同じ仕訳を月次$500で行うこともできる。正確ではあるが手間がかかる。

8.5　社債

　社債を発行して投資家から直接資金を調達する方法もある。社債の発行者は，**社債権者**と呼ばれる社債の所有者に年に1回または2回，利息を支払う。通常，調達した全額が一括で返済され，これを**社債の償還**という。社債権者は，他の投資家に社債を売却できるので，償還時の社債権者に対して最終**償還**（返済）額が支払われる。

The accounting for a bond is similar to that for a loan. If a bond was issued for $1 million and will be redeemed 5 years later for the same amount of money, the initial journal would be:

Dr	Bank	1,000,000	
Cr	Corporate bond – non-current liability		1,000,000

Interest payments would be accounted for just as for interest on a bank loan.

Also, when the time until the redemption date becomes less than one year, the liability to redeem the bond should be moved from non-current to current liabilities by a journal as follows:

Dr	Corporate bond – non-current liability	1,000,000	
Cr	Corporate bond – current liability		1,000,000

On final redemption, payment would be made from the bank account to the bondholders, removing the liability.

Dr	Corporate bond – current liability	1,000,000	
Cr	Bank		1,000,000

8.6 Corporation Tax

In most countries, there is a tax on the profits of incorporated businesses which in this book is called corporation tax. (It is also sometimes called income tax, which must not be confused with the income tax paid by individuals.) It is often one of the last entries to be made for a fiscal year, as the tax can only be finally calculated when all other entries to the profit and loss accounts have been made, and profit before tax calculated.

The tax is often payable during the **following** fiscal year. However, due to the matching principle, if profits are made during a certain fiscal year, and tax is thus payable, the tax expense must be included in that fiscal year.

Example: A company calculates its corporation tax as being $1,200 for its fiscal year ending on 31 May 2020. The tax must be paid within 3 months of the fiscal year end. What journals should be written and dated when?

Answer: A journal would be written dated 31 May 2020, as follows:

Dr	Corporation tax expense	1,200		(an income statement expense)
Cr	Corporation tax payable		1,200	(a liability in the balance sheet)

Another journal would be written dated when the tax was actually paid, to remove the liability.

社債の会計処理は借入金と同様であり，社債が$100万で発行され，5年後に同額で返済される場合の最初の仕訳は次の通り：

（借）当座預金　　　　　　　　　　1,000,000
　（貸）社債－固定負債　　　　　　　　　　　1,000,000

利払いは借入金の利息とほぼ同様。

償還日まで1年以内になった場合，次の仕訳で固定負債から流動負債へ移動

（借）社債－固定負債　　　　　　　1,000,000
　（貸）社債－流動負債　　　　　　　　　　　1,000,000

最終的な償還時には，社債権者に当座預金から支払いがなされ，消滅

（借）社債－流動負債　　　　　　　1,000,000
　（貸）当座預金　　　　　　　　　　　　　　1,000,000

8.6　法人税

　法人企業の利益に対する課税は，法人税と呼ばれる。法人税は損益勘定への他のすべての処理が行われ，税引前利益が計算された後に計算されるので，最終的な会計処理の1つである。

　法人税は次の会計年度に支払われるが，利益が一定の会計年度中に生じ，課税される場合，対応原則によって税金費用をその会計年度に含める必要がある。

例：2020年5月31に終了する会計年度に，法人税が$1,200と計算された。この税金は，会計年度末から3か月以内に支払う必要がある。

答え：2020年5月31日の仕訳

（借）法人税　　　　　　　　　　　1,200　　　　　　（損益計算書　費用）
　（貸）未払法人税　　　　　　　　　　　　1,200　　（貸借対照表　負債）

納税時の仕訳

```
Dr    Corporation tax payable   1,200
  Cr  Bank                                  1,200
```

In reality, corporation tax can be more complicated, often involving advance payments and refunds, but the simple situation described here is common for many companies.

8.7 Monthly, repeating accounting entries

There are many cases where the same journal with differing amounts has to be made every month. For example, a salaries journal or a utilities journal relating to the latest electricity bill would be needed every month in many companies.

Often exactly the same journal, including the amounts, has to be made every month. Two examples would be depreciation of a fixed asset, and repayment of a loan. For a fixed asset, the same monthly depreciation would be entered monthly until the residual amount had been reached, or the asset disposed of. For the loan repayments, if these are the same amount every month, the same journal would continue until the loan had been fully repaid.

Modern accounting systems often allow the setting up of journal entries which repeat automatically once a month, improving efficiency and accuracy.

8.8 Different journals, the same effect

Often different journals can be used to give the same effect.

In section 8.4. the monthly journal for loan principal and interest payments was shown as a four-line journal.

Alternatively, this could be shown as one payment covering both the principal and the interest, so a three-line journal with a credit to the bank account of 538.

```
Dr    Loan – current liability     500
Dr    Interest expense              38
  Cr  Bank                                     538
```

8.9 Prepayments

Businesses often make payments in advance for services to be received. The most common example is rent. A full year's insurance is often paid in advance too. The problem here is once again one of matching, so that the expense amounts are shown for the months and fiscal years when economic benefits were received, rather than when payment was made.

Example: A company has a fiscal year end of 31 December. It signs a contract on 23 October 2020 to rent and occupy an office starting from 1 November 2020. It immediately pays $3,000,

（借）未払法人税　　　　　　　　　　1,200
　（貸）当座預金　　　　　　　　　　　　　　1,200

　実務上は法人税の前払や還付もあり複雑であるが，単純化している。

8.7　月次で繰り返される会計処理

　給料や公共料金の支払いなど，毎月，異なる額で同じ仕訳をすることがよくある。減価償却や借入金の返済など，毎月，同額で同じ仕訳をすることもある。固定資産については，残存価額に達するまで，あるいは資産の処分まで，同じ月次減価償却費が毎月記入される。借入金については，毎月同額での返済の場合，完済されるまで同じ仕訳が続く。

　現代の会計システムでは，月次で繰り返す仕訳を自動設定できるので，効率性と正確性が向上している。

8.8　異なる仕訳，同じ結果

　同じ結果を得るため，異なる仕訳を使うことも多い。8.4では4行の月次仕訳が示されていたが，元利の支払をまとめて当座預金勘定の貸方に538を記入し，3行の仕訳で示すこともできる。

（借）借入金－流動負債　　　　　　　500
（借）支払利息　　　　　　　　　　　 38
　（貸）当座預金　　　　　　　　　　　　　 538

8.9　前払い

　賃借料や1年間の保険料のように，サービスを受ける際に前払いを行うことも多い。ここでも対応が問題となり，費用の額は支払われたときではなく，経済的便益を得た月と会計年度に計上される。

例：会計年度末は12月31日。2020年10月23日に，2020年11月1日から事務所を賃借する契約を結び，3か月分の家賃$3,000を前払いした。2020年の損益計算書に計上され

which is an advance payment of three months' rent. What should the rental expense relating to this office be in the 2020 profit and loss account?

Answer: The company begins to use the office from 1 November and uses it for two months, each month of rent giving an economic benefit valued at $1,000. So the 2020 profit and loss account should show $2,000, the rent for November and December. The remaining $1,000 is the rent for January 2021 and so should appear as a part of rent expenses in the 2021 profit and loss account.

The advanced payment is called a **prepayment**, and is treated as an **asset** at the time of payment, which reduces over time as the economic benefit of the expense is received.

8.10 Prepayment journals

In the example above, the following journals would be appropriate during 2020:

Dated 23 October 2020

Dr	Prepaid rent	3,000	
Cr	Bank account		3,000

Dated 1 November 2020

Dr	Rent (expense)	1,000	
Cr	Prepaid rent		1,000

Dated 1 December 2020

Dr	Rent (expense)	1,000	
Cr	Prepaid rent		1,000

This would leave a debit balance of $3,000 - 1,000 - 1,000 = 1,000$ on the prepaid rent asset account as of the end of the fiscal year on 31 December 2020.

There would be a third journal just after the new fiscal year starts, reducing the prepaid rent account to zero.

Dated 1 January 2021

Dr	Rent (expense)	1,000	
Cr	Prepaid rent		1,000

Example: a company has a fiscal year end of 31 December. On 28 September 2020 it signs an insurance contract to cover itself against natural disasters. The contract covers the two year period from 1 October 2020 to 30 September 2022. On 28 September, an immediate payment of $4,800 is made for the full contract period.

i What journal should be created on 28 September?

ii What journal would be required every month from October 2020 onwards for two years?

る家賃はいくらか？

答え：11月１日から２か月間使用し，家賃には毎月$1,000の経済的便益がある。したがって，2020年の損益計算書には11月と12月の家賃$2,000が計上される。残額$1,000は2021年１月の家賃であるから，2021年の損益計算書に計上される。

　前払高は**繰り延べ**と呼ばれ，支出時には**資産**として処理し，費用からの経済的便益の受領に応じて，時の経過とともに減少する。

8.10　前払いの仕訳

2020年の仕訳
```
2020年10月23日
  （借）前払家賃              3,000
     （貸）当座預金                       3,000
2020年11月１日
  （借）家賃（費用）          1,000
     （貸）前払家賃                       1,000
2020年12月１日
  （借）家賃（費用）          1,000
     （貸）前払家賃                       1,000
```

　この結果，2020年12月31日の決算時の前払家賃という資産勘定は，
3,000 − 1,000 − 1,000 ＝ 1,000の借方残高となる。

　新たな会計年度開始直後に3番目の仕訳を行い，前払家賃勘定はゼロになる。
```
2021年１月１日
  （借）家賃（費用）          1,000
     （貸）前払家賃                1,000
```

〔訳注〕日本では10月23日の家賃の支払時に，（借）家賃3,000（貸）当座預金3,000として費用処理し，12月31日の決算時に，資産に計上すべき額を，（借）前払家賃1,000（貸）家賃1,000とする処理法が一般的である。ただし，この設例のように月次決算の場合は，毎月末前払家賃を計上し，翌月初めにそれを元に戻す再振替と呼ばれる処理が必要となるため煩雑になる。

例：会計年度末は12月31日。2020年９月28日に災害保険契約を結んだ。補償期間は2020年10月１日から2022年９月30日の２年間であり，契約期間全体に対して$4,800を支払った。

iii What would the balance sheets and profit and loss accounts show relating to this insurance contract for 2020, 2021 and 2022?

Answer:

i Dr   Prepaid insurance   4,800

    Cr   Bank account   4,800

The payment does not provide insurance cover for September.

ii The $4,800 advance payment can be thought of as being equivalent to 24 monthly payments of $200. So each month for two years, an economic benefit of $200 is obtained. The prepaid insurance asset is reduced by $200 per month. The monthly journal would be:

Dr   Insurance   200

    Cr   Prepaid insurance   200

iii Initially an asset of $4,800 was created on 30 September.

During FY 2020: economic benefits of $200 are obtained for each of the three months from October to December, a total of $600, so the asset reduces to $4,800 - $600 = $4,200.

During FY 2021: twelve months, the full year, of economic benefit of $200 each month are obtained, so the asset reduces to $4,200 – $2,400 = $1,800.

During FY 2022: nine months of economic benefit of $200 each month are obtained, so the asset reduces to $1,800 – $1,800 = 0 by the end of September 2022.

This could be represented in a table as:

	Balance sheet	Income statement
	Prepaid insurance	Insurance expense
FY 2020	4,200	600
FY 2021	1,800	2,400
FY 2022	0	1,800

Of course, the total expense over the three fiscal years is $4,800.

Note that, if a prepayment was made as above for two years in advance, part of it should actually be treated initially as a **non-current asset** as part of the economic benefits will be received after more than one year. Financial statements often do show prepayments split into current asset and non-current asset parts.

i　9月28日の仕訳は？

ii　2020年10月以降2年間の毎月の仕訳は？

iii　2020年，2021年，2022年の保険契約について，貸借対照表と損益計算書にはどのように表示されるか？

答え：

i　（借）前払保険料　　　　　　　　4,800
　　（貸）当座預金　　　　　　　　　　　　　　4,800

この支払いは9月に関する保障を提供していない。

ii　$4,800の前払いは，$200の24月分に相当するので，2年間毎月$200の経済的便益がある。前払保険料は月次$200減少し，月次仕訳は次のとおり。

　　（借）保険料　　　　　　　　　　200
　　（貸）前払保険料　　　　　　　　　　　200

iii　9月30日当初，$4,800の資産が発生

FY2020：$200/月の経済的便益3か月分が得られたので資産は$4,200に減少

FY2021：$200/月の経済的便益12か月分が得られたので資産は$1,800に減少

FY2022：$200/月の経済的便益9か月分が得られたので資産は＄0に減少

| | 貸借対照表 | 損益計算書 |
	前払保険料	保険料
FY 2020	4,200	600
FY 2021	1,800	2,400
FY 2022	0	1,800

3年間の費用合計は$4,800

　上記のように2年分の前払いについては，その一部は当初，**固定資産**として処理する。

9 Double entry bookkeeping part 3

9.1 Inventory and Cost of Sales

When inventory is purchased, a debit entry is made to represent the inventory asset increasing, and the credit entry is normally either:

i the bank account, an asset decreases, for a cash purchase or

ii accounts payable, a liability increases, for a purchase on credit.

For a $2,000 inventory purchase, the journal would thus be:

Dr	Inventory	2,000	
Cr	Bank or Accounts payable		2,000

After sales are made, journals affecting inventory are also required to record the reduction in inventory and the increase in cost of sales (an expense).

Example: Company X sells goods for cash of $1,000. The value of the inventory sold was $800. What journals would be required?

Answer: A journal is required showing the increase in the bank account and the increase in sales.

Dr	Bank	1,000	
Cr	Sales		1,000

Another journal shows the increase in cost of sales and the decrease in inventory.

Dr	Cost of sales	800	
Cr	Inventory		800

However, cost of sales journals reducing inventory might be input after every sale, once monthly, or once yearly, depending on the method used.

9.2 Returned goods

Often customers have the right to return goods to the sellers if not satisfied, and accounting entries have to be made to reflect this.

If the customer has already paid and then the payment is refunded, the journal at the time the cash was repaid would be:

第9章 複式簿記 その3

9.1 棚卸資産と売上原価

商品購入の際，借方記入は商品，資産の増加，貸方記入は通常，次のどちらかである：

　i　当座預金からの支払による仕入れは，当座預金勘定，資産の減少
　ii　掛け仕入れについては，買掛金勘定，負債の増加

（借）商品　　　　　　　　　　　　　　　2,000
　（貸）当座預金または買掛金　　　　　　　　　2,000

〔訳注〕　inventoryは棚卸資産を意味し，小売業・卸売業では商品を，製造業では，原材料，仕掛品，製品を意味する。ここでは小売・卸売業を前提として商品とする。

商品販売の際，商品の減少と売上原価（費用）の発生を記録する仕訳も必要になる。

例：X社は$1,000で商品を販売し，代金は当座預金に入金。売り上げた商品の価額は$800であった。
答え：当座預金の増加と売上の発生

（借）当座預金　　　　　　　　　　　　1,000
　（貸）売上　　　　　　　　　　　　　　　　1,000

売上原価の発生と商品の減少

（借）売上原価　　　　　　　　　　　　800
　（貸）商品　　　　　　　　　　　　　　　　800

商品が減少し売上原価となる仕訳は，販売の都度，月次，または年次のいずれかの方法で入力する。

9.2 返品

顧客は不備のある商品を売り手に返品する権利があり，顧客が返品する。
顧客からの支払があり，返金した場合の仕訳は次の通り：

Dr   Sales – reducing the sales income account

  Cr   Bank account – assuming repayment is from the bank account

If the sale was on credit, and thus created an account receivable not yet paid by the customer, the journal would be:

Dr   Sales – reducing the sales income account

  Cr   Accounts receivable – to remove the receivable asset

If the inventory accounts had been altered too to reflect the goods being delivered, then when the goods are returned, it would also be necessary to create a journal as follows, increasing inventory as follows:

Dr   Inventory – with the value it was originally reduced by for the sale

  Cr   Cost of sales – so reduce the cost of sales

Example: On 12 August a customer buys a lawnmower for $1,200, paying immediately into the business's bank account. Also an entry of $1,000 debiting cost of sales and crediting inventory was made on 12 August. On 14 August the customer returned the lawnmower and the payment was refunded that day from the bank account. What journals are required for these transactions?

Answer: First, dated 12 August, recording the sale and the reduction in inventory, there would be the following two journals:

Dr	Bank	1,200	
Cr	Sales		1,200
Dr	Cost of sales	1,000	
Cr	Inventory		1,000

Then, dated 14 August, when the goods were returned and the payment refunded to the customer, the following two journals would be appropriate.

Dr	Sales	1,200	
Cr	Bank		1,200
Dr	Inventory	1,000	
Cr	Cost of sales		1,000

The journals dated 12 August and 14 August are equal and opposite in their effect, and have returned the inventory and sales numbers to the situation before the sale took place. However, it would **not** be acceptable to delete them, or not input either journal. Despite not changing the income statement and balance sheet (other than temporarily for two days), the transactions took place, and should be recorded.

（借）売上 – 売上勘定の減額
　（貸）当座預金 – 銀行口座からの返金の場合

掛け売り上げで，顧客がまだ支払っていなかった場合の仕訳は次の通り：

（借）売上 – 売上勘定の減額
　（貸）売掛金 – 売掛金という資産の減額

商品勘定の引き渡しも記録していた場合，次のような仕訳が必要になる：

（借）商品 – 販売によって当初減額されていた価額で
　（貸）売上原価 – 売上原価が減少するので

例：8月12日，顧客が芝刈り機を＄1,200で購入し，企業の当座預金に入金された。売上原価の借方と商品勘定の貸方に$1,000の記入も行っていた。8月14日，顧客から芝刈り機が返品され，当座預金から返金した。必要な仕訳は？

答え：8月12日，売上と商品の減少の仕訳

（借）当座預金	1,200	
（貸）売上		1,200
（借）売上原価	1,000	
（貸）商品		1,000

8月14日，商品の返品と，顧客への返金の仕訳

（借）売上	1,200	
（貸）当座預金		1,200
（借）商品	1,000	
（貸）売上原価		1,000

8月12日と14日の仕訳は，その影響が正反対となり，商品と売上が販売前の状況に戻されている。しかし，それを削除したり，仕訳を省略することはできない。2日間以外，損益計算書と貸借対照表の変化はないが，取引が行われており，記録が必要となる。

9.3 Bad debts

Normally businesses would prefer to make sales for cash rather than on credit. One reason is that with a credit sale, there is a possibility that payment will be late. There is also the possibility that the account receivable will never be paid, or only a reduced amount will be paid. There can be various reasons; two possibilities among others are disputes between sellers and buyers over the quality or condition of goods, and the bankruptcy of the buyer.

When a business considers it will never be able to collect money owing for an account receivable, and the goods will not be returned either, the account receivable is reduced. This is called **writing off** a debt. The account used is an expense account in the operating costs, called bad debt expense.

The journal would be:

Dr   Bad debt expense
  Cr   Accounts receivable

Example: Company B has an account receivable of $1,400 from company X. A payment of $300 is received and also a letter from a lawyer saying that company X has gone bankrupt, and no further payments will be made. Company B decides the remaining amount is a bad debt, and payment will never be received. What journal(s) are required?

Answer:

Dr Bank account	300		partial payment of account receivable
Cr Accounts receivable		300	
Dr Bad debt expense	1,100		judged unreceivable
Cr Accounts receivable		1,100	

Or one journal, which has the same effect:

Dr Bank account	300		partial payment of account receivable
Dr Bad debt expense	1,100		judged unreceivable
Cr Accounts receivable		1,400	now zero; partly received, partly written off

9.4 Cash and petty cash

In this section, it is now assumed that "cash" does mean **coins and banknotes only**. Although in nearly all examples and explanations in this book the assumption is that money goes in and out of bank accounts, of course cash is really used in many businesses.

Cash is an asset, and is a separate account in the accounting system, even though normally

9.3 貸し倒れ（不良債権）

　支払いが遅れる可能性があるため，掛け取引よりも現金取引が好まれる。また，売掛金が支払われない，あるいは支払額が減額される可能性もある。商品の品質や状態についての売り手と買い手の対立,買い手の倒産ということが原因として考えられる。

　売掛金が回収できないと判断され，商品も返却されない場合，債権の償却と呼ばれる売掛金の減額を行い，貸倒損失という営業費用を計上する：
　（借）貸倒損失
　　（貸）売掛金

例：X社に対して$1,400の売掛金があり$300の支払いはあったが，弁護士からX社倒産により，これ以上の支払はないと文書での連絡があった。残額を不良債権と判断した場合の仕訳は？

答え：

（借）当座預金	300		一部受領した
（貸）売掛金		300	
（借）貸倒損失	1,100		回収不能と判断
（貸）売掛金		1,100	

あるいは，同じ結果となるが：

（借）当座預金	300		一部受領した
（借）貸倒損失	1,100		回収不能と判断
（貸）売掛金		1,400	ゼロ；一部回収，一部償却

9.4 現金及び小口現金

　本節では現金は**硬貨と紙幣**だけを意味するものとする。本書のほとんどの設例と解説では，貨幣は当座預金口座での受払いを前提としているが，多くの企業において実際には現金が使用されている。
　現金は資産であり，会計システム上，独立した勘定になっている。

cash and cash equivalents are amalgamated in financial statements.

Often cash is moved to and from bank accounts, and accounting entries must be created to show that movement.

Example: A company makes a cash sale of $1,200 on 21 January. Of this, $1,000 is put in the company's bank account two days later.

What are the required journals?

Answer: Two journals are needed, as follows:

On 21 January	Dr	Cash	1,200		
	Cr	Sales		1,200	
On 23 January	Dr	Bank account	1,000		as the bank balance increases
	Cr	Cash		1,000	as the cash asset decreases

It would be very inconvenient for businesses if all purchases, even small payments such as buying stationery or postage stamps, had to be made from a bank account. Businesses often keep a small amount of cash on hand to make such payments, called **petty cash**. This too is usually a separate account in the accounting system. Businesses will withdraw more from the bank account when the petty cash balance becomes too low.

Example: A company takes $100 from its bank account to use as petty cash, and spends $25 of it on stationery. What journals are required?

Answer: Dr	Petty cash	100	
Cr	Bank account		100
Dr	Office expenses	25	
Cr	Petty cash		25

From the point of view of quality of accounting records, it is normally not a good idea to use cash for payments more often than necessary or for large sums. This is because whereas payments made through the bank account are also recorded by the bank, cash records usually have to be made completely by the business itself.

Cash is also the asset most likely to be subject to loss and theft.

In their accounting records, many businesses will have separate asset accounts for petty cash and for cash received for cash sales.

9.5 Miscellaneous income and miscellaneous expenses

Just as there are balance sheet categories called **other assets** and **other liabilities** covering assets and liabilities not falling under other categories, also many businesses have two profit and loss accounts called **miscellaneous income** and **miscellaneous expenses**. Normally they

通常，現金は当座預金口座で受け払いされ，その会計処理が必要となる。

例：1月21日，＄1,200の現金売上があり，$1,000が2日後に当座預金に入金された。必要な仕訳は？

答え：2つの仕訳が必要：

1月21日	（借）現金	1,200		
	（貸）売上		1,200	
1月23日	（借）当座預金	1,000		預金残高増加
	（貸）現金		1,000	現金資産減少

　少額の支払いを当座預金で決済するのは不便であるため，企業はその支払いのために，**小口現金**という少額の手許現金を準備している。これも会計システム上，独立した勘定となっている。小口現金の残高の減少に応じて当座預金から引き出す。

例：A社は小口現金として$100を当座預金から引き出し，そのうち$25を文房具の購入に使った。必要な仕訳は？

（借）小口現金	100	
（貸）当座預金		100
（借）事務用消耗品費	25	
（貸）小口現金		25

　現金を頻繁に多額の支払いに使用することは，会計記録の質の観点から得策ではない。当座預金からの支払いは銀行が記録するが，現金の記録は企業自身による記録が必要だからである。

　現金は紛失や盗難の可能性がもっとも高い資産であり，会計記録上，小口現金と現金売上で受け取る現金について独立した資産の勘定を設けている。

9.5　その他の収益およびその他の費用

　企業では，**雑収入**および**雑費**という2つの損益勘定を設け，他の勘定に帰属しない少額および／または異常な取引に使用される。

would be used for small amounts and/or unusual transactions not falling under any other existing account in the ledgers.

Example: An advertising agency whose offices are closed for business at weekends allows a language teacher to use its conference room on Sundays a few times a year. The teacher pays $50 in cash (actual cash) for this. What would be an appropriate journal?

Answer: Renting a conference room is not part of the main business activities. An appropriate journal would be:

Dr	Cash	50	
Cr	Miscellaneous income		50

The miscellaneous income and expense accounts might also be used for the correction of errors where it is not clear what the cause has been, and there is no other more appropriate account to use.

Example: A company has a balance in its ledger of $150 in petty cash. A staff member counts the petty cash and finds that there is $148. The reason for the error cannot be found. What should be done?

Answer: The real world takes precedence over accounting records if there is a difference. If there really is only $148 in the cashbox, then the asset account should be adjusted to that level. If there was no other more suitable account, miscellaneous expenses could be used.

The journal would be:

Dr	Miscellaneous expenses	2	
Cr	Petty cash		2

Businesses which handle a lot of cash (coins and notes) and hence do expect to have cash differences from time to time, will probably have income statement accounts for recording them, perhaps called **cash differences**.

9.6 Credit cards used for payment

A common way for both individuals and companies to make payments is using a credit card. The card company pays the vendor initially on behalf of the card user, so the user of the card then has an obligation to pay the card company, instead of the vendor. Use of the credit card thus creates a liability in the balance sheet. Periodically, often monthly, all liabilities to the card company are paid by one payment.

例：広告代理店は，年に数回，閉店時に語学講師に会議室の使用を認めており，その講師から$50の現金が支払われた。適切な仕訳は？

答え：会議室の賃貸は主たる営業活動の一部ではないため，仕訳は次の通り：
（借）現金　　　　　　　　　　　　　　50
　（貸）雑収入　　　　　　　　　　　　　　　　50

　その他の収益および費用の勘定は，誤謬の原因が不明で，適切な勘定がない場合にも使用する。

例：A社の元帳の小口現金勘定残高が$150で，従業員が数えたところ$148であり，誤謬の原因不明であった場合，どうすべきか？

答え：差異発生時は，事実が会計記録より優先される。実際に$148しかない場合，その額まで勘定を修正し，適当な科目がなければ雑費勘定を使用する。
（借）雑費　　　　　　　　　　　　　　2
　（貸）小口現金　　　　　　　　　　　　　　2

　多額の現金（硬貨と紙幣）を扱い，差異が発生した場合は，それを記録する**現金過不足**という損益計算書の勘定を設けている会社もある。

9.6　クレジットカードを使った支払

　一般的なクレジットカードを使った支払により，カード会社は利用者に代わって売り手に支払を行うため，利用者はカード会社に支払義務を負う。したがってクレジットカードの使用により貸借対照表に負債が生じる。通常，カード会社に対する毎月1回の支払によって負債が消滅する。

Example: Company X uses a credit card to pay $200 for stationery on 10 April, $350 for a hotel bill on 18 April, and $120 for insurance on 26 April. On the 20th day of every month, the full credit card bill for the **previous** month's expenditure is paid from the bank account. What journals would be required relating to these transactions?

Answer: First, three journals for each of the expenses paid would be created as follows:

Date: 10 April

Dr	Office expenses	200	
Cr	Credit card liability		200

Date: 18 April

Dr	Travel	350	
Cr	Credit card liability		350

Date: 26 April

Dr	Insurance	120	
Cr	Credit card liability		120

These three expense transactions total $670, and the whole credit card bill is then paid on 20 May from the bank account, reducing the credit card liability to zero.

Date: 20 May

Dr	Credit card liability	670	
Cr	Bank		670

例：4月10日文具代$200，4月18日ホテルの請求書$350，4月26日保険料$120の支払にクレジットカードを使用した。毎月20日，クレジットカード請求書の全額が当座預金から支払われる。必要な仕訳は？

答え：支払った各種の費用についての3つ仕訳：

4月10日（借）事務用消耗品費　　　　　　　　200
　　　　　（貸）クレジットカード未払金　　　　　　　　　　200

4月18日（借）旅費　　　　　　　　　　　　　350
　　　　　（貸）クレジットカード未払金　　　　　　　　　　350

4月26日（借）保険料　　　　　　　　　　　　120
　　　　　（貸）クレジットカード未払金　　　　　　　　　　120

　3つの取引の合計$670と，クレジットカード請求額総額が5月20日に当座預金から支払われ，クレジットカード未払金がゼロになる。

5月20日（借）クレジットカード未払金　　　　670
　　　　　（貸）当座預金　　　　　　　　　　　　　　　　　670

10.1 Trial Balance

A trial balance is a list of the balances on each account in the ledger drawn up in two columns, with debits on one side and credits on the other. In the past it was very important to create a trial balance, because with manually-created accounting records, it was quite possible that due to human error the total debits would not equal the total credits. Nowadays, computer systems have eliminated most errors that could lead to a difference between total debits and total credits. Accounting software in general does not allow the input of a journal unless the debits and credits are the same in total. However, a trial balance is still useful for many purposes. For example, by reviewing the trial balance, an accountant may realize that it is likely that some accounting entries are missing or wrong, and will do additional work.

Example: On examining the company's trial balance, an accountant notices that a fixed asset account is showing a credit balance. The accounting entries should be carefully examined for errors. Perhaps depreciation has continued being input even after net book value became zero for an asset. Perhaps a disposal has been wrongly accounted for.

10.2 Closing the accounts at the end of a financial year

Consider a company with a fiscal year ending on 30 June 2020. Here is a simple trial balance drawn up showing the balances on each account at the close of business on 30 June 2020. All the year's accounting work has been done, except the final **closing journal**.

This is a journal which transfers the closing balances from each income statement account to the retained earnings account. This has the net effect of increasing the retained earnings account by the profit for the year (or decreasing it if a loss has been made.)

Note the totals showing that the trial balance **balances**, in other words that total debits does equal total credits.

In this trial balance, the **temporary accounts** are those listed in the trial balance starting from Sales and continuing as far down as Corporation tax expense, so they must be set to zero by a closing journal.

第10章 複式簿記 その4

10.1 試算表

試算表は，借方と貸方の2つの欄で作成される元帳の各勘定残高の一覧表である。手書き簿記では人為的誤謬により，借方合計と貸方合計が一致しない可能性がかなり高かったため，試算表の作成が重要であった。現代のコンピュータシステムでは，会計ソフトが貸借同額でなければ入力を受け付けないため，そのような誤謬は生じない。しかし，試算表は依然として多くの目的に有用であり，たとえば，試算表の検証によって会計担当者は会計処理の欠落や誤謬に気づき，追加の処理を行うであろう。

例：試算表の検証で，固定資産勘定が貸方残高となっていることに気がついた。その誤謬について会計処理を慎重に調査する必要がある。資産の正味簿価がゼロになった後も減価償却が入力されていたか，処分が誤って計上されていた可能性がある。

10.2 会計年度末の決算

次頁の表は会計年度末が2020年6月30日の企業の，当日の事業終了時の残高試算表である。最終的な**決算仕訳**を除き，期中の処理はすべて終わっている。

決算仕訳は，決算残高を各損益計算書の勘定から利益剰余金勘定に振り替える仕訳であり，当期純利益には，利益剰余金を増加させる（純損失は減少させる）正味の影響がある。

この試算表の**一時的勘定**（名目勘定，期間帰属勘定）は，試算表に計上されている売上から法人税までの勘定であり，仕訳によってゼロにしなければならない。

ABC Incorporated   Trial balance as of 30 June 2020

Account	Dr	Cr
Sales		20,000
Cost of sales	14,000	
Salaries	2,000	
Advertising	500	
Rent	800	
Interest received		50
Corporation tax expense	1,000	
Bank account	4,200	
Inventory	150	
Accounts payable		550
Liability - corporation tax		1,000
Share capital		100
Retained earnings		950
Totals	22,650	22,650

This closing journal, dated the last day of the fiscal year, would be:

		Dr	Cr
Dr	Sales	20,000	
Cr	Cost of sales		14,000
Cr	Salaries		2,000
Cr	Advertising		500
Cr	Rent		800
Dr	Interest received	50	
Cr	Corporation tax expense		1,000
Cr	Retained earnings		1,750

The remaining accounts (the **permanent accounts**) from the trial balance would be used to create a balance sheet. This would give a final balance sheet for the fiscal year as follows:

ABC Incorporated   Balance sheet as of 30 June 2020

Assets		Liabilities	
Bank account	4,200	Accounts payable	550
Inventory	150	Corporation tax	1,000
		Total liabilities	1,550
		Equity	
		Share capital	100
		Retained earnings	2,700
		Total equity	2,800
Total assets	4,350	**Total liabilities and equity**	4,350

ABC株式会社　　　　　2020年6月30日時点の試算表

勘定科目	借方	貸方
売上		20,000
売上原価	14,000	
給料	2,000	
広告費	500	
賃借料	800	
受取利息		50
法人税	1,000	
当座預金	4,200	
商品	150	
買掛金		550
未払法人税		1,000
資本金		100
利益剰余金		950
合計	22,650	22,650

決算仕訳は，会計年度末の日付で次のように行われる：

（借）売上	20,000		
（貸）売上原価			14,000
（貸）給料			2,000
（貸）広告費			500
（貸）賃借料			800
（借）受取利息		50	
（貸）法人税			1,000
（貸）利益剰余金			1,750

　試算表の残りの勘定（**永久勘定，実在勘定**）は貸借対照表の作成に使用され，会計年度末の貸借対照表は次のようになる：

ABC株式会社　　2020年6月30日時点の貸借対照表

資産		負債	
当座預金	4,200	買掛金	550
商品	150	未払法人税	1,000
		負債合計	1,550
		資本	
		資本金	100
		利益剰余金	2,700
		資本合計	2,800
資産合計	4,350	**負債及び資本合計**	4,350

This would also be the balance sheet at the opening of business the next day, 1 July 2020, the beginning of the next fiscal year.

10.3 Frequency of accounting work

In a large company, staff will do accounting work every business day. In a small company, accounting may be done less frequently, perhaps a few days or even just one day per month, perhaps by company staff who do other jobs too or by external accountants. Some businesses with very few transactions might have all their accounting done in a day or less a year.

Note that even if accounting work is done quite infrequently, such as once a month or only a few times a year, transactions should be input using the date they actually occur.

10.4 Timing of accounting work

In general, accounting work takes place after transactions have happened. It may be extremely soon after, if systems are very automated, but often it will be the next day, or even longer afterwards, before some transactions are entered into the system.

There are various reasons for the delays:

i Transactions may occur after accounting staff have finished their day's work, or on days they are not at work.

ii There may be delays in receiving information. Invoices and bills for expenses may not be received for some time after the end of a month or fiscal year.

iii A large volume of transactions and/or a low level of staffing may mean that accounting staff usually or always have a backlog of unperformed work.

iv If external accountants are used, they are usually working for many clients simultaneously, and so may do their work days, weeks or even months after transactions have taken place.

Also, time is used for checking that the accounting work is correct and complete. This is particularly true for the financial statements produced after the fiscal year end.

Example: A multinational with a fiscal year ending on 30 September 2020, might not finalize its accounting for that fiscal year until late October, November or even later.

Note however, that whereas the final accounting work would be carried out in say October or November, the **transaction dates in the accounting system** for FY 2020 would all be between 1 October 2019 and 30 September 2020.

これは，次年度2020年7月1日の開始貸借対照表でもある。

10.3　会計処理の頻度

　大企業では担当者が毎日会計処理を行うが，中小企業では月に数日ないし1日，他の業務も行う従業員や外部の会計士が行うこともある。取引が非常に少ない企業では，会計処理が1日であるいは年内に終わることもある。会計処理が月に1回等であっても，実際に取引が行われた日付で入力しなければならない。

10.4　会計処理のタイミング

　会計処理は取引の発生後に行われ，システムが自動化されている場合はその直後になり，多くの場合，取引がシステムに入力されるのは翌日以降になる。

　この遅れにはいくつか理由がある：

i　会計担当者の業務終了後や休暇日に取引が発生する。

ii　納品書や経費請求書の受け取りが，月末や年度末後となるなど，情報入手の遅延がある。

iii　多数の取引，および／または少ない担当者数は，会計担当者が残務を抱えていることを意味する。

iv　外部の会計士を使っている場合，彼らは多忙なため，取引後，数日，数週間ないし数か月後に会計処理を行うこともある。

例：会計年度末が2020年9月30日の多国籍企業は，10月下旬，11月以降まで会計処理が終わらないことがある。決算が10月や11月に行われても，2020会計年度の**会計システム上の取引日**は，2019年10月1日から2020年9月30日までの間になる。

10.5 Viewing accounting information

An individual accounting entry can best be understood by looking at a journal entry. This will show the date, which accounts were debited and credited, by how much and an explanation of what the transaction was.

However, people doing accounting work often wish to examine one account in detail, so for example, to know such things as:

i what the current balance (the total) of the account is, and

ii whether the accounting entries made to that account seem correct and complete.

It would be very inconvenient and time-consuming to try to investigate i and ii above by looking at a list of journals, as there could be hundreds or thousands of journals during a fiscal year, most of which do not relate to the account in question.

Matters such as i and ii above are best checked by looking at the "page" of the ledger (or with accounting software, the screen representing this page) showing one account only.

The contents displayed depend on the computer system being used, but might normally show, at the top of the page, details about which fiscal year the accounting data relates to, and the account name.

Then, for each accounting entry there would be a line showing:

a the transaction date of the entry,

b the other account used in the journal,

c some explanation about the transaction,

d separate columns showing each debit and credit amount, and

e a running total showing the balance on the account.

Each account in the balance sheet (or permanent account) would start with the final balance from the previous fiscal year as its opening balance. Each profit and loss account (or temporary account) would start from zero at the beginning of the fiscal year. Examples of account pages are as follows, for a company whose fiscal year begins on 1 April 2020.

10.5 会計情報を見る

個々の会計処理は仕訳を見れば理解できる。仕訳には，日付，借方記入と貸方記入された勘定，金額，摘要が示されている。

しかし，会計処理の担当者は次の事項を知るために１つの勘定を精査する：
i 勘定の現在の残高（合計）
ii 会計年度中に勘定が正確かつ完全に処理されているかどうか

会計年度中に数百，数千の仕訳が存在する可能性があり，その多くが当該勘定に関連していないため，仕訳の一覧をみて上記 i，ii を調査するのは煩雑で時間もかかる。

上記 i， ii の事項は，元帳の「ページ」（または画面）を見てチェックすることが最善である。

表示内容はコンピュータシステムによって異なるが，ページの上部に会計データが関係する会計年度の詳細と勘定科目が表示される。
そして，会計処理が罫線で区分されている。
a 記載日
b 仕訳の相手勘定
c 取引の摘要
d 借方，貸方の金額欄
e 勘定残高を示す合計

貸借対照表の各勘定（永久勘定）は，前年度末残高を期首残高として開始する。各損益勘定（一時的勘定，期間帰属勘定）は，各年度期首にゼロで開始する。2020年4月1日に会計年度が始まる会社の勘定のページを以下に示す：

Example 1: The bank account

Account name: Bank account						Fiscal year: 2021

Month	Day	Other account	Description	Dr	Cr	Balance
April	1		Balance from previous year			24,321
April	3	Accounts payable	ZZZ Inc., invoice 145		473	23,848
April	4	Office expenses	Stationery purchased		264	23,584
April	7	Accounts receivable	John Smith, invoice 2018-3	6,950		30,534
April	8	Sales	Paulson Incorporated	1,000		31,534
April	10	Salaries liability	March staff salaries		8,455	23,079
April	11	Interest receivable	Interest on account	32		23,111
April	12	Inventory	DDD Limited		500	22,611

As it is a balance sheet account, the bank account has a non-zero balance on 1 April, $24,321, which was the final amount at the end of the previous fiscal year. There are then typical examples of amounts paid into the bank account (the debit column) and amounts paid from the bank account (the credit column). On each line at the right-hand side the balance column shows the current balance after that transaction. For example, the last line shows a balance of $22,611, which represents the amount in the bank account as of 12 April, a debit balance as it is an asset.

Example 2: The utilities account

Account name: Utilities						Fiscal year: 2021

Month	Day	Other account	Description	Dr	Cr	Balance
April	30	Accounts payable	Electric company, April	890		890
April	30	Accounts payable	Water company, April	110		1,000
May	31	Accounts payable	Electric company, May	925		1,925
May	31	Accounts payable	Water company, May	102		2,027

As this is an income statement account, it begins from zero on 1 April.

Each month there are entries showing the value of the electricity and water used during that month. The credit entry each time is to accounts payable, as the utilities suppliers will be paid in arrears. Utilities expenses have reached $2,027 by 31 May, a debit balance as it is an expense.

例 1 ： 当座預金勘定

			勘定科目：当座預金		会計年度：2021	

月	日	勘定科目	摘要	借方	貸方	残高
4	1		前期繰越			24,321
4	3	買掛金	ZZZ社, 送り状 145		473	23,848
4	4	事務用消耗品費	文房具購入		264	23,584
4	7	売掛金	John Smith, 送り状 2018-3	6,950		30,534
4	8	売上	Paulson社	1,000		31,534
4	10	給料	3月従業員給料		8,455	23,079
4	11	受取利息	口座の利息	32		23,111
4	12	商品	DDD 社		500	22,611

　貸借対照表の勘定であるから，4月1日の残高はゼロではなく前年度期末残高の$24,321となる。当座預金勘定への入金額（借方欄）と出金額（貸方欄）の典型例がある。残高欄には取引後の残高が示される。最終行の残高は4月12日時点の当座預金の資産としての借方残高である。

〔訳注〕accounts payableは未払金であるが，わが国の商品売買業では，頻繁に変動する商品代金の未払高については，買掛金としてその他の未払金とは区別する。

例 2 ： 水道光熱費勘定

			勘定科目：水道光熱費		会計年度：2021	

月	日	勘定科目	摘要	借方	貸方	残高
4	30	未払金	電力事業者, 4月分	890		890
4	30	未払金	水道事業者, 4月分	110		1,000
5	31	未払金	電力事業者, 5月分	925		1,925
5	31	未払金	水道事業者, 5月分	102		2,027

　損益計算書の勘定であるからゼロで始まる。毎月，その月に使用した水道光熱費が計上されている。貸方記入は後払いであるため未払金となる。水道光熱費は5月31日までに$2,027となり，費用の勘定であるから借方残高となる。

Example 3: The equipment account from fixed assets

Account name: Fixed assets - equipment					Fiscal year: 2021	

Month	Day	Other account	Description	Dr	Cr	Balance
April	1		Balance from previous year			16,000
April	30	Depreciation	April depreciation		800	15,200
May	31	Depreciation	May depreciation		800	14,400
June	18	Accounts payable	5 tables, GHI Furniture Ltd	1,200		15,600
June	30	Depreciation	June depreciation		820	14,780

This account is a balance sheet account, and so it begins with the net book value of equipment brought forward from the end of the previous financial year, $16,000. Each month end, a depreciation entry is made, reducing the value of the equipment assets and increasing the depreciation expense account. Some new assets, five tables, are bought on credit on 18 June, and so the monthly depreciation amount increases slightly from June. The net book value of the equipment is a debit balance of $14,780, a debit balance as this is an asset account.

Example 4: The sales account

Account name: Sales					Fiscal year: 2021	

Month	Day	Other account	Description	Dr	Cr	Balance
April	3	Accounts receivable	Mary Tudor		1,500	1,500
April	5	Accounts receivable	Luigi Italian Restaurant		852	2,352
April	8	Bank	Paulson Incorporated		1,000	3,352
April	10	Accounts receivable	XYZ partners		3,300	6,652

As this is an income statement account, it too begins from zero on 1 April. There are three sales on credit which also increase accounts receivable. There is one sale for cash on 8 April; the debit side of this entry can be seen in the bank account shown above. Sales income has reached $6,652 by 10 April. This is a credit balance as it is revenue.

10.6 Review of accounting work

It is very important to do accounting work as accurately as possible. Even though computerized systems can reduce the frequency of errors, they cannot be entirely eliminated.
It was mentioned already that trial balances are reviewed for errors. However, trial balances show account totals, and an examination of totals only will not reveal all errors. Accounting

例 3 ：固定資産の備品勘定

勘定科目：固定資産－備品			会計年度：2021			
月	日	勘定科目	摘要	借方	貸方	残高
4	1	∗	前期繰越			16,000
4	30	減価償却費	4月減価償却		800	15,200
5	31	減価償却費	5月減価償却		800	14,400
6	18	未払金	テーブル5脚, GHI家具会社	1,200		15,600
6	30	減価償却費	6月減価償却		820	14,780

　貸借対照表の勘定であるから前会計年度末繰越の備品の正味簿価$16,000で始まる。毎月末，減価償却の記入が行われ，備品の価額が減少し，減価償却費が増加する。6月18日に新たな資産が後払いで購入されたので，月次減価償却費が5月より増加している。備品の正味簿価は借方残高$14,780で，資産の勘定であるから借方残高となる。

例 4 ：売上勘定

勘定科目：売上			会計年度：2021			
月	日	勘定科目	摘要	借方	貸方	残高
4	3	売掛金	Mary Tudor		1,500	1,500
4	5	売掛金	Luigi Italian Restaurant		852	2,352
4	8	当座預金	Paulson Incorporated		1,000	3,352
4	10	売掛金	XYZ partners		3,300	6,652

　損益計算書の勘定であるからゼロで始まる。売掛金が増加した3件の掛け売り上げがある。1件の当座預金売り上げがある；この記入の借方側は当座預金勘定に計上されている。収益の勘定であるから貸方残高となる。

10.6　会計処理の検証

　会計処理を正確に行うことが重要で，コンピュータシステムで誤謬を減らすことはできても，すべての排除はできない。誤謬を検証する試算表には勘定の合計額が表示されるが，合計額の検証だけでは誤謬のすべては明らかにはならない。会計担当者は記入が完全かつ正確であるかをチェックするために，勘定ごとに元帳のページを検証

staff will usually review the pages of the ledger account by account to check the entries seem complete and correct. Anything which seems unusual should be investigated, and if it is indeed an error, a correction will be made.

Example: An accountant reviews the January to June fixed asset - equipment page for errors in a company's ledger. What, if anything, looks as though it may be wrong and why?

Account name: fixed assets - equipment				Fiscal year: 2021		

Month	Day	Other account	Description	Dr	Cr	Balance
		....	....			26,522
January	31	Depreciation	January depreciation		300	26,222
February	28	Depreciation	February depreciation		300	25,922
March	31	Depreciation	March depreciation	300		26,222
April	30	Depreciation	April depreciation		300	25,922
May	14	Bank	Cutting machine purchase	2,800		28,722
May	31	Depreciation	May depreciation		300	28,422
June	30	Depreciation	June depreciation		300	28,122

Answer: As would be expected, there is a monthly journal for depreciation, reducing the asset value. Also a fixed asset has been purchased on 14 May, which is not unusual. However, there appear to be two problems.

i) March depreciation is a debit entry, increasing the asset balance instead of decreasing it, so it appears likely that the debits and credits have been confused in the March journal, and it needs corrected.

ii) Although a new machine has been bought in May, the May and June depreciation figures are still 300. Normally a fixed asset purchase would mean the monthly depreciation amount increases.

The accountant should investigate these two entries further.

Note that although an accounting entry may appear doubtful, it could be correct. For example, perhaps the machine bought on 14 May will not be commence to be used until July or August, and so it has been decided that its depreciation entries will only start from then.

している。異常とみられるものはすべて調査し，誤謬があった場合は訂正される。

例：元帳の誤謬について，１月から６月までの固定資産‐備品ページを検証した。誤謬があるとすれば何か，そしてその理由は？

| | | | 勘定科目：固定資産‐備品 | | 会計年度：2021 | | |

月	日	勘定科目	摘要	借方	貸方	残高
		....	....			26,522
1	31	減価償却費	1月減価償却		300	26,222
2	28	減価償却費	2月減価償却		300	25,922
3	31	減価償却費	3月減価償却	300		26,222
4	30	減価償却費	4月減価償却		300	25,922
5	14	当座預金	裁断機購入	2,800		28,722
5	31	減価償却費	5月減価償却		300	28,422
6	30	減価償却費	6月減価償却		300	28,122

答え：予想通り，減価償却の月次仕訳があり，また５月14日に固定資産を購入しているが異常なことではない。ただし，２つ問題がある。

i　３月の減価償却では資産の減少ではなく増加となっているため，仕訳の借方と貸方を間違っている可能性があり，修正する必要がある。

ii　５月に新しい機械を購入しているが，５月と６月の減価償却費が300のままである。固定資産の購入は月次の減価償却費を増加させる。

　会計担当者はこの２つの記入をさらに調査しなければならない。

　会計処理に疑義があっても正しい場合もある。５月14日に購入した機械は，７月，８月から使い始めるため，減価償却の記入はその時点から開始することもある。

10.7 Error correction in later fiscal periods

If accounting records are properly reviewed, normally errors can be discovered quite quickly and corrected in the fiscal period they occur, thus not causing any errors in the annual financial statements. In fact the time (which can be weeks or months) between the end of a business's fiscal year and the publishing of its financial statements is a key period for especially thorough checking, and mistakes can still be corrected at this time.

Unfortunately, errors are sometimes only found **after issue** of the financial statements, during the next fiscal year. Unless these are large and significant errors, the financial statements will normally **not** be altered and re-issued. Corrections will normally be made in the accounting records of the financial year during which the errors are discovered.

Example: Company C has a fiscal year ending on 31 December 2020. The company misfiles its November electricity bill of $332, and so no accounting entry is made in 2020 relating to it. The financial statements are published on 4 February 2021. The electricity supplier points out non-payment of the November bill, and company C pays the bill in March 2021. What should be done?

Answer: The amount is not large, so the financial statments will not be re-issued, nor will the 2020 accounting records be altered. A debit entry of $332 will be made to utilities in March 2021. So actually utilities as shown in the 2020 income statement will be $332 too low, and in the 2021 income statement the number will be $332 too high. However, such small errors are preferred to the time and trouble required to re-issue financial statements.

10.8 T accounts

T-accounts are useful as a way of showing the flow of transactions through an account. They can also be used to calculate the balance on an account. Here is example showing the bank account.

Balance b.f. means balance brought forward, in other words the final balance from the previous period, whether a month or a year.

Balance c.f. means balance carried forward, in other words the closing balance, which will be the opening balance in the following period, whether a month or a year.

10.7 事後の会計期間における誤謬の訂正

　会計記録を厳密に検証すれば，誤謬は迅速に発見され，発生した期間中に訂正されるため，年次財務諸表に誤謬は生じない。企業の会計年度末と財務諸表公表まで（数週間ないし数か月）に徹底したチェックが入り，その時点で訂正できる。

　残念ながら，財務諸表**公表後**に誤謬が見つかることもある。誤謬が多額で重要でない場合には財務諸表は変更せず再公表されない。その訂正は，誤謬が見つかった会計年度の会計記録で行われる。

例：2020年12月31日が会計年度末のC社が，11月の電気料金請求書$332を誤ってファイルしていたため，その会計処理が2020年に行われず，財務諸表は2021年2月4日に公表された。事業者から11月の未払いが指摘され，C社は2021年3月にその請求額を支払った。どうすべきか？

答え：金額が大きくないので，財務諸表は再公表されず，2020年の会計記録も変更されない。2021年3月に水道光熱費の借方に$332記録される。したがって，2020年の損益計算書に計上される水道光熱費は$332少なくなり，2021年は$332多くなるが，このような少額の誤謬は，財務諸表公表の時間と手間よりも望ましい。

10.8 T勘定

　T勘定は，取引の流れを明らかにする有用な方法で，勘定の残高の計算にも利用できる。

　前期繰越（b.f.）は繰り越された残高，月または年度の前期末残高を意味する。

　次期繰越（c.f.）は繰り越す残高，月または年度の翌期首残高を意味する。

Bank

Debit			Credit		
Date	**Account**	**Amount**	**Date**	**Account**	**Amount**
Aug 1	Balance b.f.	12,500	Aug 7	Rent	3,800
Aug 3	Sales	1,200	Aug 21	Accounts payable	3,430
Aug 9	Accounts receivable	3,220	Aug 21	Petty cash	500
Aug 13	Interest received	100	Aug 26	Salaries	2,810
			Aug 29	Bank loan	1,500

Debits are shown on the left, credits on the right.

The date column shows the transaction date.

The account column shows the other part of the journal for this transaction. For example, the entry on 3 August shows that corresponding to the 1,200 debit in the bank account, there was an equal and opposite entry (a credit) of 1,200 made to sales.

The amount is the monetary amount of the transaction.

T-accounts can also be used to give the account balance. This is done by first totaling the debits and the credits, and writing the larger of the two as the total at the bottom – in this case 17,020 from the debit column.

Bank

Debit			Credit		
Date	**Account**	**Amount**	**Date**	**Account**	**Amount**
1 Aug	Balance b.f.	12,500	7 Aug	Rent	3,800
3 Aug	Sales	1,200	21 Aug	Accounts payable	3,430
9 Aug	Accounts receivable	3,220	21 Aug	Petty cash	500
13 Aug	Interest received	100	26 Aug	Salaries	2,810
			29 Aug	Bank loan	1,500
Total		17,020	Total		17,020

The next step is to put in the balancing figure in the column required to give the same total on both sides. In this case it is 4,980 in the credit column. This number is the account balance.

当座預金

	借方			貸方	
日付	勘定科目	金額	日付	勘定科目	金額
8/ 1	前月繰越	12,500	8/ 7	賃借料	3,800
8/ 3	売上	1,200	8/21	買掛金	3,430
8/ 9	売掛金	3,220	8/21	小口現金	500
8/13	受取利息	100	8/26	給料	2,810
			8/29	借入金	1,500

　借方を左側，貸方を右側に示し，日付欄は取引日，勘定科目欄は取引の仕訳の相手勘定を示す。8月3日は，当座預金の借方1,200に対応するのが，売上への1,200の反対（貸方）記入となる。金額欄は取引価額である。

　T勘定は勘定残高の計算にも利用できる。まず借方と貸方を合計し，2つのうち大きい方を最終行に合計として記入する－この場合は借方欄から17,020。

当座預金

	借方			貸方	
日付	勘定科目	金額	日付	勘定科目	金額
8/ 1	前月繰越	12,500	8/ 7	賃借料	3,800
8/ 3	売上	1,200	8/21	買掛金	3,430
8/ 9	売掛金	3,220	8/21	小口現金	500
8/13	受取利息	100	8/26	給料	2,810
			8/29	借入金	1,500
合計		17,020	合計		17,020

次に両側の合計が一致するように，残高の数値を挿入する。この場合は貸方欄に4,980，この数値が勘定残高となる。

Bank

Debit			Credit		
Date	**Account**	**Amount**	**Date**	**Account**	**Amount**
1 Aug	Balance b.f.	12,500	7 Aug	Rent	3,800
3 Aug	Sales	1,200	21 Aug	Accounts payable	3,430
9 Aug	Accounts receivable	3,220	21 Aug	Petty cash	500
13 Aug	Interest received	100	26 Aug	Salaries	2,810
			29 Aug	Bank loan	1,500
			31 Aug	Balance c.f.	4,980
Total		17,020	Total		17,020

Because the number required to make both totals equal was in the credit column, this means the overall balance is actually a debit balance.

Here is an example using the sales account. The balance carried forward means the total on the sales account as of 30 September. The sales account shows various sales made for cash or on credit.

Sales

Debit			Credit		
Date	**Account**	**Amount**	**Date**	**Account**	**Amount**
			1 Oct	Balance b.f.	1,200
			6 Oct	Bank	1,500
			8 Oct	Accounts receivable	2,300
			10 Oct	Bank	500
			21 Oct	Accounts receivable	400
31 Oct	Balance c.f.	6,100	22 Oct	Accounts receivable	200
Total		6,100	Total		6,100

The balancing amount required to make both totals equal was a 6,100 debit, so there is a 6,100 credit balance on the account.

T-accounts are often used in a simpler form, for example without dates, to illustrate accounting entries in a format that is easy to understand.

当座預金

借方			貸方		
日付	勘定科目	金額	日付	勘定科目	金額
8/ 1	前月繰越	12,500	8/ 7	賃借料	3,800
8/ 3	売上	1,200	8/21	買掛金	3,430
8/ 9	売掛金	3,220	8/21	小口現金	500
8/13	受取利息	100	8/26	給料	2,810
			8/29	借入金	1,500
			8/31	次月繰越	4,980
合計		17,020	合計		17,020

　両者の合計を等しくするために必要な数値は貸方欄にあったので，全体としての残高は借方残高であることを意味する。

　下記の売上勘定の前月繰越は，9月31日時点の売上勘定の総額を意味する。

売上

借方			貸方		
日付	勘定科目	金額	日付	勘定科目	金額
			10/ 1	前月繰越	1,200
			10/ 6	当座預金	1,500
			10/ 8	売掛金	2,300
			10/10	当座預金	500
			10/21	売掛金	400
10/31	次月繰越	6,100	10/22	売掛金	200
合計		6,100	合計		6,100

　貸借合計を一致させるために必要な額は6,100の借方であるから，この勘定には6,100貸方残高がある。

　T勘定は，会計処理をわかりやすく示すために，日付を省略して利用されることも多い。

Example: Use simple T accounts, without dates, to show the following information and series of transactions.

i The bank account has a balance brought forward of $3,200, and accounts payable has a balance brought forward of $950.

ii A utilities bill of $100 is received.

iii The account payable of $950 is fully paid.

iv There is a cash sale of $800

Answer:

Bank

Balance b.f.	3,200	Accounts payable	950
Sales	800	Balance c.f.	3,050
	4,000		4,000

Accounts payable

Bank	950	Balance b.f.	950
Balance c.f.	100	Utilities	100
	1,050		1,050

Sales

Balance c.f.	800	Bank	800
	800		800

Utilities

Accounts payable	100	Balance c.f.	100
	100		100

例：日付なしのＴ勘定で，以下の情報と一連の取引を示しなさい。

i 当座預金勘定の残高は$3,200，未払金勘定の残高は$950であった。

ii 公共料金の請求書＄100を受領した。

iii $950の未払金を全額支払った。

iv 当座預金売上が$800であった。

答え：

当座預金

前月繰越	3,200	未払金	950
売上	800	次月繰越	3,050
	4,000		4,000

未払金

当座預金	950	前月繰越	950
次月繰越	100	公共料金	100
	4,000		4,000

売上

次月繰越	800	当座預金	800
	800		800

公共料金

未払金	100	次月繰越	100
	100		100

Chapter 11 Ratio analysis

11.1 Users of financial statements

A company's financial statements are potentially of interest to various outsiders. Examples are:

i) Investors (both existing and potential) in the company's shares, and advisors who give advice relating to such investments.

ii) Providers of finance, such as banks making loans. This includes both banks which have lent money to the company already, and banks making a decision whether or not to provide finance.

iii) Providers of goods and services, who may wish to assess the ability of a business to properly carry out a transaction. A wholesaler providing goods on credit, for example, would like to assess whether a retailer seems to have the financial strength to pay for the goods fully and on time, particularly for large orders.

iv) Government departments, such as tax authorities, regulators and statisticians.

As well as reading the financial statements, many users will wish to analyze the figures and perform various calculations using them, for example to indicate whether or not a business seems to be financially healthy and performing well.

11.2 Overview of ratio analysis

One key method used is ratio analysis, where one number from the financial statements is divided by another, and its value and meaning considered.

An example of a simple ratio is cost of sales divided by sales. So, if during FY 2020, cost of sales was $9,000, and sales was $12,000, then the ratio, expressed as a percentage, would be 75%.

Businesses normally want the ratio of cost of sales to sales to be as low as possible, as this gives a higher gross profit. However, one ratio alone gives only limited information. Other numbers to use for comparison are needed. Without them it is impossible to answer such important questions as whether 75% represents a good, average or poor performance, or whether the situation is improving, remaining about the same or becoming worse.

第**11**章 比率分析

11.1 財務諸表の利用者

さまざまな外部関係者が財務諸表に関心がある。

例：

ⅰ）株式への現在および潜在的投資家，投資アドバイザー

ⅱ）銀行などの資金提供者

　　すでに資金提供している銀行，資金提供の意思決定をしている銀行

ⅲ）財・サービスの提供者

　　卸売業者は小売業者が全額かつ期限内に支払う財務的能力を評価

ⅳ）課税庁，規制機関，統計局などの政府部門

　多くの利用者は，例えば企業が財務的に健全で好業績であるかを明らかにするために，財務諸表を読むだけでなく，数値を分析し，さまざまな計算をしたいと考えている。

11.2 比率分析の概要

財務諸表の数値を他の数値で割り，価値と意味を検討。

例：売上高売上原価率75% ＝ 売上原価$9,000 ÷ 売上高$12,000

　売上原価率↘　→　売上総利益↗

　比較のためには他の数値を利用し，75%が良いのか，平均的なのか，劣っているのか，あるいは状況が改善しているのか，現状維持なのか，悪化しているのかを検討。

Two main methods of comparison are used to analyze ratios more meaningfully.

1) **Comparison over time:** This is calculating ratios using the financial statements for the same business for two or more financial years, which shows whether the ratios are improving or becoming worse.

2) **Comparison to other businesses:** Financial statements are obtained from various businesses, and the ratios compared. Depending on the purposes of the analysis, this might often be ratios for businesses operating in similar markets, or ratios based on averages for certain business sectors.

Note that a company's management will often find ratio analysis taken from financial statements of limited use. This is because financial statements only shows information available to outsiders, whereas the management would normally have access to more detailed information from within the company.

However, management will often still be interested in the impression being given to outsiders by the financial statements and the ratios they show. They can, for example, affect the share price.

11.3 Types of ratios used in analysis

Ratios can be classified depending on the type of information they give. One such system of classification divides ratios into four types as follows:

1 **Liquidity ratios**, which measure the business's short-term financial health, showing its ability to pay financial obligations as they become due.

2 **Solvency ratios**, which examine borrowings, equity and earnings to assess the longer-term financial health of a business.

3 **Profitability ratios**, which look at the level of profits generated by a business compared to its levels of assets and expenses.

4 **Efficiency ratios,** which evaluate how well a company uses its assets to generate sales and maximize profits.

In studying the ratios, it is important to understand what information they are giving, whether high or low ratios are better, and what the unit being used is.

11.4 Liquidity ratios

The word **liquidity** is used here to mean a business being able to have access to sufficient cash with sufficient speed. The ability to pay its debts as they fall due is very important for any business. In the worst scenario, liquidity problems could lead to bankruptcy. Even without

比率分析の 2 つの方法
1) **期間比較**：同一企業の2事業年度以上の財務諸表を使って比率計算
2) **企業間比較**：同業他社の比率，業界平均値を使って比率を比較

　財務諸表は外部関係者に利用可能な情報だけを表示しているのに対し，経営者は，内部のより詳細な情報にアクセスできる。そのため，経営者は，比率分析は限られた用途の財務諸表から得られていることをわかっている。

　しかし，経営者は財務諸表が外部関係者に与える印象と比率に関心があり，株価に影響を与える可能性もある。

11.3　分析で使用される比率の種類

提供する情報の種類による分類
1　**流動性比率**：企業の短期的な財務健全性を測定，支払期日到来時の金融負債の支払能力を明らかにする。
2　**支払能力比率**：企業の長期的な財務健全性を評価，借入金，資本および収益を調査。
3　**収益性比率**：資産および費用に対する利益の水準を調査。
4　**効率性比率**：売上を生み出し，利益を最大化するために資産をうまく活用しているかを評価。

　どのような情報を提供しているのか，高い比率がいいのか低い比率がいいのか，使用されている単位は何かを理解することが重要。

11.4　流動性比率

　流動性とは，企業が十分な資金を十分なスピードで入手できることを意味する。債務の返済期限到来時の支払能力は，どの企業にとっても非常に重要であり，最悪のシナリオでは，破産につながる可能性もある。延滞によって，取引先が消極的になった

going bankrupt, frequent late payment can also affect a business negatively. Other businesses may become reluctant to trade with it, or they may insist on stricter conditions, such as advance payment of goods ordered. Fines could be incurred if taxes are paid late.

To indicate if a business seems to have enough liquidity or not, liquidity ratios such as this one are used:

current ratio = current assets ÷ current liabilities

This simple ratio is used to measure the company's ability to pay its short-term obligations as they fall due. It assumes that current assets either already are cash, or can be turned into cash and used to pay the current liabilities. Clearly a high ratio is better than a low one.

In many businesses it would be thought that a ratio of at least 1 and preferably substantially higher, should be maintained. However, to some extent it also depends on what exactly is contained in current assets and current liabilities.

Sometimes the number **current assets – current liabilities**, known as **working capital**, is also calculated, showing in money what the surplus or deficit of current assets compared to current liabilities is.

Example: Company A has the following balance sheet numbers for three fiscal years. Calculate and comment on its current ratio.

End of fiscal year	2018	2019	2020
Cash and cash equivalents	37,841	39,651	46,854
Marketable securities	21,500	21,800	22,000
Inventories	37,487	39,111	77,045
Accounts receivable	12,409	16,821	5,611
Prepayments	16,343	17,650	15,561
Other current assets	1,990	2,011	4,222
Total current assets	127,570	137,044	171,293
Total current liabilities	82,356	96,542	112,439

Answer: the calculations are as follows.

End of fiscal year	2018	2019	2020
Current ratio	1.5	1.4	1.5

Although the balance sheet has increased in size greatly over the three years, the current ratio has remained very stable. After a slight decline in 2019, the 2020 ratio has recovered to the

り，代金の前払いなどの厳しい条件を要求されたり，税金の滞納は罰金が科されるなど，企業に悪影響を与えることもある。流動性比率は，企業に十分な流動性があるかを明らかにするために使用される。

流動比率＝流動資産÷流動負債

これは，負債の支払期限到来時の短期支払能力を測定するための比率で，流動資産がすでに現金になっているか，現金になり流動負債を支払うために使用されると仮定しており，高い比率の方が良い。

少なくとも1以上の比率を維持すべきであるとされているが，ある程度までは流動資産と流動負債の内容にもよる。

運転資本＝流動資産－流動負債

これは，流動負債と比較した流動資産の過不足額を明らかにする。

例：A社の3事業年度の貸借対照表は次のとおり。
流動比率を計算し，コメントしなさい。

事業年度末	2018	2019	2020
現金及び現金同等物	37,841	39,651	46,854
有価証券	21,500	21,800	22,000
棚卸資産	37,487	39,111	77,045
売上債権	12,409	16,821	5,611
前払費用	16,343	17,650	15,561
その他の流動資産	1,990	2,011	4,222
流動資産合計	127,570	137,044	171,293
流動負債合計	82,356	96,542	112,439

答え：計算結果

事業年度末	2018	2019	2020
流動比率	1.5	1.4	1.5

貸借対照表のサイズは3年間でかなり拡大したが，流動比率は非常に安定している。2020年度の若干の減少後，2020年度の比率は2018年度の水準に回復している。およそ

2018 level. At around 1.5, the current ratio does not necessarily indicate liquidity problems.

11.5 Limitations of analysis using the current ratio

The current ratio assumes that all current assets can be turned into cash with acceptable speed, and at the monetary value shown in the balance sheet. This may not always be true. For example, it may be difficult to sell certain items of inventory quickly, or not at the full price, especially if quick sale is desired. Some inventory may even be unsaleable. Also, some current assets may be impossible to turn into cash by their nature. Prepaid rent will often be an example of this – once paid, it usually cannot be returned. The next ratio – the acid test - adjusts for these current asset issues.

acid test ratio =(cash and cash equivalents + marketable securities + accounts receivable) ÷ current liabilities

This ratio is a more severe test of liquidity than the current ratio, as the numerator has been reduced by only including some current assets, but the denominator is unchanged, still including all current liabilities. It is also often called the **quick ratio.**

Securities means financial instruments such as bonds and shares held by the company. **Marketable** means that they can be bought and sold on a public bond or stock exchange. Thus for the purposes of the acid test it is assumed that such assets can be turned in cash easily and quickly, and at a known price.

A good reason for using the more pessimistic acid test ratio is that whereas having some excess liquidity is usually not a problem, having too little liquidity could be very serious.

Example: using the numbers in the above example, use the acid test to analyze and comment on company A's liquidity situation. Compare it to the results obtained using the current ratio. **Answer**: the calculations are as follows.

End of fiscal year	2018	2019	2020
Acid test ratio	0.9	0.8	0.7

To show in detail how the ratio is calculated using the 2018 numbers:

numerator = cash and cash equivalents + marketable securities + accounts receivable

$= 37,841 + 21,500 + 12,409 = 71,750$

denominator = 82,356 (total current liabilities)

acid test ratio = $71,750 \div 82,356 = 0.9$

The results show that the liquidity situation is actually deteriorating as the balance sheet grows. Between 2018 and 2020 it has fallen from 0.9 to 0.7, so compared to the current ratio, the acid

1.5の流動比率は必ずしも流動性の問題になるとは限らない。

11.5　流動比率分析の限界

　流動比率は，すべての流動資産が貸借対照評価額で現金に転換することを前提としているが,棚卸資産の特定品目は販売困難かもしれないし,即時に販売が必要な場合,定価販売は難しかったり，販売できなかったりするものもある。また，前払家賃などの流動資産は現金に転換されない。次の当座比率（酸性試験比率）*は，この流動資産の問題に対処している。
＊日本では，当座比率という呼称が一般的である。

当座比率＝（現金及び現金同等物＋市場性ある有価証券＋売上債権）÷流動負債

　当座比率は，分母をすべての流動負債のまま変更せず，分子に一部の流動資産のみを算入することによって，流動比率よりも厳しい流動性のテストを行うものである。

　有価証券：会社が保有する社債および株式などの金融商品
　市場性：公債または証券取引所で売買可能であること
　当座比率では，このような資産が容易かつ即座に既定の価格で現金に転換できることが前提とされている。
　ある程度の過剰な流動性は問題にはならないが，過少な流動性は深刻な問題になる可能性があるために，悲観的な当座比率が使用されている。
　例：上記の例を利用し，A社の流動性の状況について当座比率を使って分析し，コメントしなさい。その結果を流動比率と比較しなさい。
　答え：計算結果

事業年度末	2018	2019	2020
当座比率	0.9	0.8	0.7

　2018の数値を使って計算過程を示すと：
　分子＝現金及び現金同等物＋市場性ある有価証券＋売上債権
　　＝　37,841　＋　21,500　＋　12,409　＝　71,750
　分母＝82,356（流動負債合計）
　当座比率＝71,750÷82,356＝0.9
　当座比率は2018年度から2020年度の間，0.9から0.7まで低下しており，貸借対照表は成長しているが，年次の比率と傾向の両面で流動性はかなり悪化していることが明

test shows a much worse situation, both in terms of the annual ratios and the trend.

On closer examination of the current assets, it can be seen that the cause is a large increase in inventory as a proportion of current assets. There could be liquidity problems if this inventory proves difficult to sell, or has to have its price reduced to sell it.

11.6 Solvency ratios

Solvency ratios also examine the balance sheet, but from a longer-term point of view to look at the financial health and funding of the business.

One way of thinking about a balance sheet is that the asset side shows the resources being used to run the business, whereas the liability side shows that these assets are being financed in two ways, either by liabilities or from the part belonging to the owners, the equity.

The balance sheet is based on the accounting equation,

Assets = Liabilities + Equity

Assets can thus only increase if either i) liabilities increase or ii) equity increases.

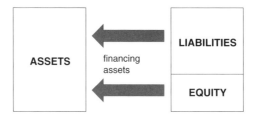

So businesses are being partly financed internally, from the amounts paid for share capital and from retained earnings, and partly externally, from liabilities.

The first solvency ratio examines the ratio between these two different ways of financing. There are various possible definitions of debt. The one used here is **all liabilities**. This means that **any liability** is considered a form of debt, not only formal borrowing arrangements such as bank loans or corporate bonds issued. This is because there is a future obligation to make a payment for something already received, such as inventory obtained on credit, the supply of electricity, or work done by employees paid in arrears.

debt to equity ratio = liabilities ÷ equity

A high ratio would imply that the business is very dependent on external finance, rather than internal finance. This would normally mean more of a need for the company to make regular interest and principal payments. Clearly an inability to make these payments could threaten the

らかになった。

　その原因は流動資産のうち棚卸資産の割合の大幅な増加にあり，販売が難しい，あるいは販売のために値下げをしなければならない場合，流動性の問題が生じる可能性がある。

11.6　支払能力比率

　支払能力比率も貸借対照表を検討するものであるが，長期的な視点から企業の財務健全性と資金調達をみるものである。

　貸借対照表では，資産側に事業の運営に使用されている資源が示されているのに対して，負債側に，負債と資本という資産の調達方法が示されていると考えることができる。

　貸借対照表は，次の会計等式に基づいている。

資産＝負債＋資本

　資産は，ⅰ）負債が増加，あるいはⅱ）資本が増加する場合にだけ増加する。

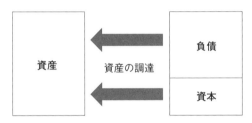

　このように，企業は払込資本と留保利益の額から内部的に，負債から外部的に資金調達を行っている。

　最初の支払能力の比率は，この２つの異なる資金調達方法の比率に関するものである。ここでは債務を負債と定義し，借入金や社債だけでなく，買掛金，未払電力料，未払給与など，すでに受け取った何らかのものに対する将来の支払い義務も含む。

負債比率＝負債÷資本

　この比率が高い場合には，企業が外部資金に大きく依存し，定期的な元利の支払いを行う必要があることを意味する。この支払いができないことは会社の存在を脅かし，将来の事業拡張に投資するどころか，元利の支払いに多額の現金が使われることも意味する。

　逆に，株主には資本の払い戻しを要求する権利がないので，低い比率の方が安全である。また，留保利益は株主への配当に使用されるが，一定水準の配当を要求する権

existence of the company. It also means that excess cash may have to be used to make interest and principal payments, instead of being invested in future expansion of the business.

Conversely, a low ratio is normally safer, because shareholders do not have the right to demand the return of the share capital paid into the company. Also, retained earnings may be used to pay dividends to shareholders, but again there is usually no right to demand dividends of a certain level.

Example: use the following numbers to analyze and comment on the debt to equity ratio for companies A, B and C.

Balance sheet	A Inc.	B Inc.	C Inc.
Total assets	4,211	77,000	82,462
Bank loans (current part)	500	8,481	25,331
Other current liabilities	1,722	7,612	1,477
Bank loans (non-current part)	400	32,661	34,989
Corporate bond			12,000
Other non-current liabilities	82	45	1,300
Total liabilities	2,704	48,799	75,097
Equity	1,507	28,201	7,365

Answer:

Company	A Inc.	B Inc.	C Inc.
Debt to equity ratio	1.8	1.7	10.2

All three companies are mainly financed by debt rather than equity. However, for A and B, the equity part is proportionally much larger, whereas C is very largely financed by external debt. Thus although in balance sheet size, B and C are similar, as regards debt to equity ratio, A and B are similar.

A bank manager will often look at this ratio to help make a decision on giving further loans. It might be considered that C Inc. is already too dependent on external funding, and no further loans should be given. Assuming similar profitability, it may seem safer to lend to A Inc. or B. Inc.

利はない。

例:以下の数値を使って，A社，B社，C社の負債比率を分析し，コメントしなさい。

貸借対照表	A社	B社	C社
資産合計	4,211	77,000	82,462
借入金（流動項目）	500	8,481	25,331
その他の流動負債	1,722	7,612	1,477
借入金（固定項目）	400	32,661	34,989
社債			12,000
その他の固定負債	82	45	1,300
負債合計	2,704	48,799	75,097
資本	1,507	28,201	7,365

答え：

会社	A社	B社	C社
負債比率	1.8	1.7	10.2

　3社はすべて，資本よりも債務で資金調達を行っている。しかし，A社とB社については資本の割合がかなり大きいのに対して，C社は大部分を外部の債務で資金調達している。貸借対照表のサイズはB社とC社が近似しているが，負債比率はA社とB社が近似している。

　C社は外部融資に依存しすぎており，追加の融資は行われず，収益性が同様だと仮定すると，A社かB社に融資する方が安全であると考えられる。

11.7 Leverage

It would be too simplistic to say that a very low debt to equity ratio is good and a high one is bad.

Consider two new businesses, X and Y. The owners of X and Y each have $4,000 to invest as share capital in their newly incorporated companies.

X initially obtains a bank loan of $1,000 and issues share capital of $4,000, and thus initially has the amount of $5,000 in its bank account. Its debt to equity ratio is 0.25.

Y initially obtains a bank loan of $40,000 and issues share capital of $4,000 and thus initially has the amount of $44,000 in its bank account. Then its debt to equity ratio is 10.

Clearly, X has a much lower debt to equity ratio, and seems more safely financed.

However, it can also be seen that Y now has the potential to expand its business much more easily. For example, it could pay cash to buy a machine for $10,000, or inventory for $8,000, whereas X cannot do either of these things, without somehow obtaining more money.

So for the same initial investment, the owners of company Y have the potential to create a larger business.

This concept where a business uses outside finance to obtain capital to expand is called leverage. (It comes from the idea that a lever can be used to allow a small force to move a large, heavy object.) Company Y is said to be **highly leveraged** compared to company X.

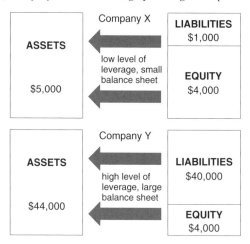

So rather than the lower the better, businesses should have an appropriate debt to equity ratio.

Companies with the need to own expensive fixed assets often have higher debt to equity ratios (i.e. are highly leveraged) as even a large and successful business may not have enough cash

11.7 レバレッジ

　負債比率が低い方が健全で高い方が不健全というのはあまりに単純すぎる。X社とY社という2つの新規企業で考えてみよう。X社は銀行から＄1,000の融資を受け，＄4,000で株式を発行し，銀行に$5,000の預金がある。負債比率は0.25となる。Y社は銀行から$40,000の融資を受け，$4,000で株式を発行し，銀行に$44,000の預金がある。負債比率は10となる。X社の負債比率のほうがかなり低く，安全に資金調達をしているように思える。

　しかし，Y社のほうが簡単に事業を拡張できる可能性があるのに対して，X社は，たとえば$10,000の機械や$8,000の棚卸資産の購入しようとしても，さらに資金を獲得しなければ，どちらも購入できない。

　Y社の所有者は，同じ初期投資について，より大きな事業を展開する可能性をもっている。

　企業が事業拡張のための資本を獲得するために外部資金を利用する概念は，レバレッジと呼ばれる（梃子を使い，小さな力で大きく重い物体を動かすことができる考えに由来）。Y社はX社よりも**レバレッジが高い**といえる。

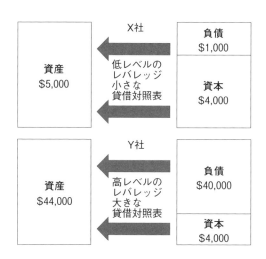

　このように負債比率は低い方が望ましいというよりもむしろ，適切な負債比率をもつべきである。大規模で成功している企業であっても，追加借入を行わなければ高額な固定資産の支払いを行うための十分な現金及び現金同等物を保有していないため，

and cash equivalents to pay for such assets without additional borrowing. These companies hope that the assets bought will generate profits, and the cash from the profits can be used over time to repay the debts incurred.

Debt to equity ratio using borrowing only

Another definition of debt can be used to calculate a slightly different ratio.

In this case, debt is considered only to be formal borrowing arrangements, such as short-term and long-term bank loans (the most common item) and corporate bonds issued (usually for larger companies only).

Example: using this definition of debt as formal borrowings only, calculate the debt to equity ratio for A. Inc., B Inc., and C Inc., using the numbers in the balance sheet above.

Answer: the calculations are as follows:

Company	A Inc.	B Inc.	C Inc.
Debt (borrowings only)	900	41,142	72,320
Equity	1,507	28,201	7,365
Debt to equity ratio	0.6	1.5	9.8

This measure omits liabilities which are not borrowing arrangements, but it too shows that C Inc. is much more dependent on external financing.

Another solvency ratio is the **total assets to debt ratio**. This shows how reliant the company is on debt (liabilities) to finance its assets.

The ratio is calculated as (total assets)÷(total liabilities)

Example: calculate the total assets to debt ratio for A Inc., B Inc. and C Inc. above.

Answer: as below

Company	A Inc.	B Inc.	C Inc.
Assets	4,211	77,000	82,462
Liabilities	2,704	48,799	75,097
Assets to debt ratio	1.6	1.6	1.1

Once more, although the balance sheet sizes of B and C are similar, A and B have much more similar ratios, showing a similar financing structure. C has greater reliance on debt to finance its assets.

多くの場合，高い負債比率になっている（レバレッジが高い）。購入した資産が利益を生み，利益からもたらされる現金を債務の返済に使用することができる。

借入金だけを使った負債比率

　債務として，短期及び長期の銀行ローンと社債といった正式な借入契約があるものだけを考慮し，別の比率を計算する。

例：正規の借入金として，この債務の定義を使い，A社，B社，C社の負債比率を前掲の貸借対照表の数値を利用して計算しなさい。
答え：計算結果は以下のとおり

会社	A社	B社	C社
負債（借入金のみ）	900	41,142	72,320
資本	1,507	28,201	7,365
負債比率	0.6	1.5	9.8

　この尺度は，借入契約のない負債を除外しているが，C社はより多くの外部資金調達に依存していることも明らかにしている。

　その他の支払能力比率である**総資産負債比率**は，会社が資産を調達するために，どれくらい債務（負債）に依存しているのかを明らかにする。
　この比率は，**（資産合計）÷（負債合計）**として計算される。

例：前掲のA社，B社，C社の総資産負債比率を計算しなさい。
答え：以下のとおり

会社	A社	B社	C社
資産	4,211	77,000	82,462
負債	2,704	48,799	75,097
資産負債比率	1.6	1.6	1.1

　B社とC社の貸借対照表のサイズは同規模であるが，A社とB社の比率のほうが同様の比率になっており，同様の資金調達構造となっている。C社のほうが，資産の調達を債務に依存している。

Related to these solvency ratios is the **interest coverage ratio**. This is normally calculated by adding back interest paid to obtain a figure called earnings before interest and tax (EBIT) , and then comparing this figure to the amount of interest payable on debts. This shows how many times the earnings of the company can pay for interest owing.

interest cover ratio = (earnings before interest and tax)÷interest expense

The ratio is expressed as the number of times interest can be paid for from earnings before interest and tax. A high ratio is better.

Example: using the numbers below for company Q, calculate and comment on its interest coverage ratio.

Fiscal year	2018	2019	2020
Interest expenses	2,420	2,790	3,367
Profit before tax	4,681	4,899	5,312

Answer: as below.

Fiscal year	2018	2019	2020
Profit before tax	4,681	4,899	5,312
Add back interest expenses	2,420	2,790	3,367
Profit before interest and tax	7,101	7,689	8,679
Interest cover (times)	2.9	2.8	2.6

This shows that although profits are increasing, interest payments are increasing even faster and so the interest cover is slowly declining.

11.8 Profitability ratios

One common ratio used to measure profitability is:

return on assets (ROA) = (Profit × 100) ÷ Average total assets

The profit figure used could be that before or after tax, depending on what one desires to measure. A percentage is calculated. The higher the percentage, the better, as the available assets are being used more efficiently to generate profits.

支払能力に関連する**インタレスト・カバレッジ・レシオ**は，支払利息を戻し入れて加算した利払及び税引前利益（EBIT）と呼ばれる数値を，支払利息額と比較して計算する。

インタレスト・カバレッジ・レシオ＝利払及び税引前利益÷支払利息

この比率は支払利息が利払及び税引前利益から支払われた倍数として示され，高い方が良い。

例：Q社の以下の数値を使って，インタレスト・カバレッジ・レシオを計算し，コメントしなさい。

事業年度	2018	2019	2020
支払利息	2,420	2,790	3,367
利払前利益	4,681	4,899	5,312

答え：

事業年度	2018	2019	2020
支払利息	4,681	4,899	5,312
支払利息の戻入れ	2,420	2,790	3,367
利払前税引前利益	7,101	7,689	8,679
インタレストカバレッジ（倍）	2.9	2.8	2.6

増益となっているが，支払利息がそれ以上に増加しているため，インタレストカバレッジが低下している。

11.8　収益性比率

収益性を測定する一般的な比率：

総資本利益率*（ROA）＝利益×100÷総資産平均値

使用する利益は，何を測定したいかによって税引前または税引後となる。利用可能な資産が利益をより効率的に生み出しているということなので，比率が高いほうが，良い。

＊直訳すると資産利益率であるが，日本では総資本利益率と呼ぶことが多い。

Example: calculate the return on assets for two companies, A and B, from the following information, and comment on the results.

Company A	At 31 December	2018	2019	2020
	Total assets	273	282	273
	Total equity	122	145	171
	Profit after tax	23	26	28
Company B	At 31 December	2018	2019	2020
	Total assets	344	359	357
	Total equity	88	116	144
	Profit after tax	21	28	29

Answer: as below. Note that using average assets for each year means that the 2018 ROA cannot be calculated as there are no 2017 asset numbers provided.

Return on assets (%)	Fiscal year	2019	2020
	Company A	9.4	10.1
	Company B	8.0	8.1

Both companies improved their return on assets between 2019 and 2020. Although B is generating larger profits, A is using its assets more efficiently.

Note that average total assets is used, for two reasons.

i The profit was generated by the assets in use during the entire financial year, not only by those existing at the end of the financial year.

ii It may be that the final balance sheet assets total is temporarily lower or higher than normal, so using an average should give a better measure.

Another measure of overall company profitability from the point of view of the shareholders is:

Return on Equity (ROE) = (Profit × 100) ÷ Average equity

Once more a percentage is calculated and the higher it is, the better.

Example: calculate the return on equity for the two companies, A and B, from the information used in the previous example, and comment on the results.

例：次の情報に基づき，A社，B社，2社の総資本利益率を計算し，計算結果について
てコメントしなさい。

A社	12月31日	2018	2019	2020
	資産合計	273	282	273
	資本合計	122	145	171
	税引後利益	23	26	28
B社	12月31日	2018	2019	2020
	資産合計	344	359	357
	資本合計	88	116	144
	税引後利益	21	28	29

答え：資産平均値を使うということは，2018年度のROAは2017年度の資産の数値が
なければ計算できないことを意味することに注意。

総資本利益率（%）	事業年度	2019	2020
	A社	9.4	10.1
	B社	8.0	8.1

　両社ともに総資本利益率が改善している。Bの方が多額の利益を生み出しているが，
Aの方が資産を効率的に使っている。

　利益は事業年度末の資産だけでなく事業年度にわたって使用する資産から生み出さ
れ，最終的な資産は，一時的に低い数値や高い数値になっている可能性もあるため，
平均値を使用する。

　株主の視点からの会社全体の収益性に関する指標：

自己資本利益率（ROE）＝利益×100÷自己資本平均値

これも高い方が良い。

例：前の設例で使用した情報から，A社とB社，2社の自己資本利益率を計算し，計
算結果についてコメントしなさい。

Answer: The calculation results are as below.

Return on equity (%)	Fiscal year	2019	2020
	Company A	19.5	17.7
	Company B	27.5	22.3

This time the results are rather different. For both companies, return on equity is falling.

Also company B's structure, with less of its financing coming from equity, means it has a much better return on equity than company A.

The equity, composed of amounts invested in the business as share capital, and the retained earnings that remain in the business, could in theory be used for some other investment. The ROE calculation is asking whether, by using them in this business, the percentage obtained as profit is adequate, and also whether it is improving or not.

Other profitability measures concentrate on the profit and loss account.

Net profit margin

Businesses are interested in the percentage of sales which finally becomes profit after all expenses are considered, and clearly the higher this is, the better.

net profit margin (%) = (profit × 100) ÷ sales

Gross profit margin

The concept of gross profit, sales minus cost of sales, has already been seen as part of the profit and loss account. The gross profit margin divides gross profit by sales and expresses the number as a percentage. Once more, the higher this is, the better.

gross profit margin (%) = (sales – cost of sales) × 100 ÷ sales

This ratio helps show businesses whether there is or is not a sufficient difference between the direct costs of goods, and their sales price.

Operating expenses ratio

This ratio examines how the expenses of operating the business compare to sales.

operating expenses ratio = (operating expenses × 100) ÷ sales

Again, the higher the ratio, the better. Businesses wish to make sure not only that sufficient gross profit is being made, but also that the percentage of sales proceeds being used to generally run the business is not excessive.

答え：

自己資本利益率（％）	事業年度	2019	2020
	A社	19.5	17.7
	B社	27.5	22.3

　両社ともに自己資本利益率が低下しているが，自己資本による調達が少ないB社の資本構成も，A社より自己資本利益率が優れていることを意味する。

　払込資本と留保利益で構成される自己資本は，理論上，他の投資に使用することが可能である。ROEは，それらを事業活動に使用して，利益として得られた割合が十分かどうか，また，改善されたかどうかを明らかにする。

　損益計算書によるその他の収益性の指標：

当期純利益率＝当期純利益×100÷売上高

高い方が良い。

売上高総利益率＝（売上高－売上原価）×100÷売上高

高い方が良い。商品の直接原価と販売価格との間に十分なさやがあるかを明らかにする。

営業費率（販売費及び一般管理費率）＝営業費（販管費）×100÷売上高

営業費率は低い方が良い。十分な粗利(売上総利益)を獲得できているだけでなく，売上高が事業の一般的な運営に使用される割合が過剰ではないことを確認したいと望む。

Earnings per share

A ratio of interest to shareholders, often shown at the bottom of the income statement, is

earnings per share = profit ÷ number of shares

This shows the amount of profit which in theory belongs to each share. Once more, the higher this is, the better. It is expressed in currency units, so, for example, dollars or yen or euros per share.

Example: Use the numbers below to calculate i) net profit margin, ii) gross profit margin, iii) operating expenses ratio, and iv) earnings per share for companies C and D, and comment on the results.

Year ending 31 March	Units : $	2019	2020
Company C	Sales	3,420	3,828
	Cost of goods sold	1,200	1,291
	Operating expenses	1,660	1,741
	Profit after tax	462	663
	Number of shares	800	1,400
Company D	Sales	2,880	3,250
	Cost of goods sold	984	1,002
	Operating expenses	1,710	1,850
	Profit after tax	125	161
	Number of shares	120	120

Answer: The calculations are as follows.

	Year ending 31 March	2019	2020
Company C	Gross profit margin (%)	65	66
	Operating expenses ratio (%)	49	45
	Net profit margin (%)	14	17
	Earnings per share ($)	0.6	0.5
Company D	Gross profit margin (%)	66	69
	Operating expenses ratio (%)	59	57
	Net profit margin (%)	4	5
	Earnings per share ($)	1.0	1.3

i Net profit margins for both C and D have improved slightly over the two years. However, C has a much higher net profit margin, meaning it is more successful at retaining a higher

一株当たり利益（EPS）＝純利益÷株式数

理論上，各株式に帰属する利益の額を示し，高い方が良い。この指標は，一株当たりのドル，円，ユーロなどの貨幣単位で表示する。

例：以下の数値を使って，C社とD社のⅰ）純利益率，ⅱ）売上高総利益率，ⅲ）営業費率，ならびにⅳ）一株当たり純利益を計算し，結果についてコメントしなさい。

3月31日に終了する年度　単位：$		2019	2020
C社	売上高	3,420	3,828
	売上原価	1,200	1,291
	営業費	1,660	1,741
	税引後利益	462	663
	発行済株式数	800	1,400
D社	売上高	2,880	3,250
	売上原価	984	1,002
	営業費	1,710	1,850
	税引後利益	125	161
	発行済株式数	120	120

答え：

	3月31日に終了する年度	2019	2020
C社	売上高総利益率（%）	65	66
	営業費率（%）	49	45
	純利益率（%）	14	17
	一株当たり利益（$）	0.6	0.5
D社	売上高総利益率（%）	66	69
	営業費率（%）	59	57
	純利益率（%）	4	5
	一株当たり利益（$）	1	1.3

ⅰ）C社とD社の純利益率は，2年間でわずかに改善しているが，C社の純利益率のほうがかなり高く，高い最終的な利益率を維持しており，成功しているといえる。

percentage of sales as final profit.

ii The gross profit margins are improving slightly for both C and D, and are quite similar.

iii It can be seen from the operating expenses ratio that C has a much lower percentage, and hence a lower ratio of running costs compared to sales than D. Thus the large difference in net profit margin is being caused by higher running costs relative to sales in D.

iv Despite ratios i and iii above being poorer, D shows rather better earnings per share than C, due to the fewer shares it has issued. Thus, normally it would be expected that D's share price would be higher than C's.

Note also that despite its results improving, C's earnings per share went down, as it had 600 more shares at the end of 2020. This shows that although a new share issue will bring in more money to a company, it also has the effect of reducing earnings per share, and hence perhaps share price.

There are in fact many other profitability ratios which can be calculated and which may or may not be of interest to companies depending on what kind of business they operate in. For example, some businesses may wish to examine ratios relating to salaries costs to see if they seem acceptable.

11.9 Efficiency ratios

There are various ratios used to measure the efficiency that a business uses its assets in its activities.

Inventory turnover ratio

Consider two companies selling similar products, and the following facts over the fiscal year 2020.

Fiscal year 2020	Average inventory	Cost of goods sold
Company A	1,000	3,500
Company B	1,100	5,500

Inventory is of similar size in both companies, but it seems goods are passing in to and out of B's inventory at a greater speed. Sales are taking place faster, which is good as inventory is converted into either accounts receivable or cash more quickly.

The **inventory turnover ratio** measures this speed, and is calculated as:

inventory turnover ratio = cost of goods sold ÷ average inventory

This shows the **number of times** the equivalent value of the whole average inventory is sold

ⅱ）　Ｃ社とＤ社の売上高総利益率はわずかに改善し，かなり近似している。

ⅲ）　営業費率については，Ｃ社はかなり高い比率となっており，Ｄ社より売上高に対するランニングコストの比率が低いことがわかる。純利益率の大きな違いは，Ｄ社のランニングコストの高さに原因がある。

ⅳ）　上記ⅰとⅲが低調という比率に反して，Ｄ社は発行済み株式数が少ないことにより，一株当たり利益はＣ社より優れている。したがって，Ｄ社の株価の方が，Ｃ社より高くなるであろう。

　業績の改善にもかかわらず，2020年度末までにさらに600株を発行したため，Ｃ社の一株当たり利益は減少していることにも注意が必要である。新株の発行が会社にさらに資金をもたらすものの，一株当たり利益が減少し，そしておそらく株価にも影響するであろう。

　他にも計算可能な多くの収益性比率があり，たとえば，ある企業は，給与が許容範囲か高すぎるかを検討するために，給与に関する比率を調査するかもしれない。

11.9　効率性比率

　企業が諸活動に資産を使用する効率性を測定するために，さまざまな比率が使われている。

棚卸資産回転率

　類似品を販売している２社の2020年度の状況。

2020事業年度	棚卸資産（平均）	売上原価
Ａ社	1,000	3,500
Ｂ社	1,100	5,500

　両社とも在庫は同程度であるが，Ｂ社の棚卸資産のほうが速いスピードで入出庫しており，より速い販売によって，棚卸資産が迅速に売掛金や現金に転換している。

棚卸資産回転率＝売上原価÷棚卸資産平均値

　Ａ社：3,500÷1,000＝3.5回
　Ｂ社：5,500÷1,100＝5回
　Ｂ社のほうが効率的に運営されている。回転数は高いほうが良い。

in a year.

Company A's ratio is (3,500 ÷ 1,000) = 3.5 times

Company B's ratio is (5,500 ÷ 1,100) = 5 times

B is operating more efficiently. The higher the number of times inventory is turned over, the better.

Another ratio often calculated, which essentially uses the same information and presents it differently is the **average number of days in inventory**, calculated as:

average number of days in inventory = 365 × (average inventory ÷ cost of goods)

This is thus just 365÷inventory turnover ratio.

Using the numbers above:

Company A: (365÷3.5) = 104 days

Company B: (365÷5) = 73 days

This means that A takes 104 days to sell the equivalent value of the average inventory it has, whereas B only requires 73 days. The lower the number of days goods are in inventory, the better, so B is performing better.

The faster the cycle, the better…

Normally average inventory is calculated from two balance sheets, as closing inventory for the previous financial year equals opening inventory for the current financial year. For example, for fiscal year 2020:

Average inventory FY2020 = (inventory FY 2019 + inventory FY 2020)÷2

Different industry sectors

Businesses operating in different industry sectors often have completely different turnover ratios.

Example 1: A dealer in used cars normally has about 50 vehicles valued at $1,000 each on

同じ情報を使った**棚卸資産平均回転日数**という別の比率もある。

　　棚卸資産平均回転日数＝365×（棚卸資産平均値÷売上原価）

　　　　　　　　　　　　　＝365÷棚卸資産回転率

A社：365÷3.5＝104日

B社：365÷5＝73日

　A社が平均在庫を販売するのに104日かかっているのに対して，B社は73日しか要していないということを意味している。在庫日数は短いほうが良いのでB社のほうが上手く運営されている。

サイクルが速いほうが良い…

　前期末の棚卸資産と当期首の棚卸資産は同じなので，棚卸資産平均値は2期分の貸借対照表から計算する。

業種による違い

　業種の違いによって，回転率はかなり異なっている。

例1：中古車のディーラーは平均的な在庫として＄1,000で評価した車両およそ50台を保有し，年間100台の販売を見込んでいる。

average in inventory and expects to sell about 100 cars a year.

inventory turnover ratio $= (100 \times 1,000) \div (50 \times 1,000) = 2$

Example 2: A retailer of food which is only fresh enough to sell at full price for about a week would want an inventory turnover ratio of 50 or more.

How much inventory should be held?

Businesses do not know exactly what their future sales will be, so very often they will either have too much or too little inventory.

Too little inventory of an item means sometimes losing sales, as customers may decide they cannot or do not want to wait until the item is available.

However, too much inventory also brings various problems. These are:

i Extra warehousing costs are incurred

ii Liquidity becomes poorer, as suppliers of inventory may have to be paid before the goods are sold, so cash outflow takes place before cash inflow

iii Goods may become unsaleable, or have to be sold cheaply, because they become too old (e.g. food), go out of fashion (e.g. clothes) or become technologically out of date (e.g. electronic goods.)

Receivables turnover

When companies sell on credit, it is preferable that the customer pays as soon as possible. Slow payments cause various problems including:

Cash shortages for the seller: The seller will often already have paid for the production or purchase of the goods, so a long delay before receiving payment for accounts receivable means outflows of cash may take place substantially before inflows, leading to liquidity problems.

Eventual non-payment: In the worst scenario, the customer could go bankrupt before payment.

Thus sellers on credit want to measure if large amounts of accounts receivable are building up, and how quickly customers are paying.

Consider two companies of similar size, which are selling goods on credit.

Fiscal year 2020	Average ARs	Sales on credit
Company C	3,500	70,000
Company D	8,000	72,000

These companies might examine the receivables turnover ratio, which is:

receivables turnover ratio = sales on credit ÷ average accounts receivable

Company C: 70,000 ÷ 3,500 = 20 times

棚卸資産回転率＝（100×1,000）÷（50×1,000）＝2

例2：およそ1週間で定価販売する新鮮な食品の小売業者は，棚卸資産回転率が50回以上必要である。

在庫はどのくらい保有すべきか？

　将来どのくらいの売上があるか正確にはわからないため，在庫は過剰か過少のどちらかになることが多い。

　過少在庫は，顧客が入荷まで待てないかもしれないので，売り上げを失うことがあることを意味する。

　しかし，過剰在庫にも以下の問題がある：

ⅰ）追加の保管料が発生する。

ⅱ）商品販売前に仕入代金を前払しなければならないので流動性が悪化する。

ⅲ）商品の悪化（例：食品），流行遅れ（例：衣料品），新技術の登場（例：電子機器）によって，商品が売れなくなったり，安く売らなければならないおそれがある。

売上債権回転率

　会社は売掛金を顧客が迅速に支払うことを望んでいる。支払いの遅れは以下の問題を引き起こす：

売り手の資金不足：売り手は仕入代金を支払っているので，売掛金の回収の遅れは流動性の問題につながる。

最終的な未払：最悪のシナリオは顧客の倒産である。

　売り手は多額の売掛金が滞留していないか，顧客が迅速に支払うかを測定したいと考えている。

　同規模の2社が掛けで商品を販売しているとしよう。

2020事業年度	売掛金（平均）	掛け売上高
C社	3,500	70,000
D社	8,000	72,000

　売上債権回転率＝掛け売上高÷売掛金平均値

　C社：70,000÷3,500＝20回

　D社：72,000÷8,000＝9回

Company D: 72,000 ÷ 8,000 = 9 times

The ratio is showing that on average, company C completes the process from making a sale to receiving payment 20 times a year, whereas company D only achieves this 9 times a year. Company C is operating more efficiently. The higher the number of times credit sales are turned in money received, the better.

This data too has an alternative way of being used in a calculation. This is called the average collection period, showing how many days it takes on average from making a credit sale to receiving the money.

average collection period = 365 × (average accounts receivable÷sales on credit)

or,

average collection period = 365 ÷ receivables turnover

Using the numbers above:

Company C: (365÷20) = 18 days

Company D: (365÷9) = 41 days

On average, company D is taking much longer to collect money from credit sales, so is operating less efficiently than company C in this respect.

The faster the cycle, the better…

Normally average accounts receivable is calculated from two balance sheets, as closing accounts receivable for the previous financial year equals opening accounts receivable for the current financial year. For example, for fiscal year 2020:

Average ARs FY2020 = (ARs FY 2019 + ARs FY 2020)÷2

Sales on credit are being used in the calculation, not total sales, because cash sales are never part of accounts receivable.

C社が販売から代金回収までのプロセスを年平均20回完了しているのに対して，D社は年平均9回達成していることが示されており，C社のほうが，事業運営は効率的である。売掛金を現金となる回転数が高いほど良い。

平均回収期間と呼ばれる別の計算方法もあり，平均して何日で売掛金が回収されたかを示すものである。

平均回収期間＝365×（売掛金平均値÷掛け売上高）

あるいは

平均回収期間＝365÷売上債権回転率

C社：365÷20＝18日

D社：365÷9＝41日

平均すると，D社は売掛金を回収するのにかなり長期間を要しており，C社より事業運営が効率的ではない。

サイクルが速いほうが良い…

前期末売掛金と当期首売掛金は同じなので，売掛金平均値は，2期分の貸借対照表から計算する。

FY2020売掛金平均値＝（FY2019売掛金＋FY2020売掛金）÷2

現金売上は売掛金にはならないので，計算に当たり，売上高合計ではなく掛け売上高を使用する。

11.10 Problems with and limitations of ratio analysis across different businesses

There are various potential problems and limitations, such as:

a It is often difficult to say what a good or bad ratio is, especially where business sectors are different.

Example: For goods sold in large quantities and at quite low prices, where inventory turnover is fast, a low gross margin – just a few percent, for example – may be acceptable. A seller of used cars, who sells only a few a week, and must have substantial inventory on hand, would probably not find that enough.

b Companies will often have different fiscal years. This could make results difficult to interpret, and also lead to various different and subjective methods of analysis.

Suppose the fiscal year end of company A is 30 June, whereas the fiscal year end of company B is 31 December.

Should A's ratios for the year ending 30 June 2020 be compared with B's ratios for the year ending 31 December 2019 or 31 December 2020? Or should an average of the two be calculated? Thus, there are at least three different methods, which may all give very different results.

c Companies will often only be competitors for some of their products. So company A may sell computer software and provide computer consulting services, whereas B may sell computer software and hardware.

d Mergers and acquisitions may complicate matters. Suppose the average annual sales growth in an industry during 2020 was about 5%, but a company, A, increased its sales during 2020 by 20%. At first this may look like an excellent performance. However, what if at the beginning of 2020, A acquired a competitor, B, and that 2020 sales relating to B's customers were included in A's total? Perhaps A's large sales growth is purely due to acquiring B and adding its sales to A's own. In this case further analysis (if suitable information is available) would be needed before drawing a conclusion on A's performance.

e Different accounting methods may be in use. Company A may depreciate factory equipment over 3 years, whereas company B depreciates similar equipment over 5 years.

11.10 異なる事業間の比率分析に関する問題と限界

潜在的問題と限界

a 業種が異なる場合，比率の良し悪しを判断するのは難しいことが多い。
例：大量に低価格で商品を販売すると，棚卸資産回転が速くなり，売上総利益率が低くなることは許容されるかもしれない。一週間に数台しか販売せず，相当量の在庫を必要とする中古車の売り手は，それで十分だとは判断しないであろう。

b 事業年度が異なる場合，結果の解釈が困難になり，多種多様で主観的な分析方法となってしまう。

A社の決算日が6月30日，B社が12月31日であると想定する。この場合，A社の2020年6月30日に終了する会計年度の比率は，B社の2019年12月31日に終了する会計年度と2020年12月31日に終了する会計年度のどちらの比率と比較すべきなのか？2年間の平均値を計算すべきなのか？3つの異なる方法が存在し，結果に大きな違いが出るかもしれない。

c 多くの場合，製品の一部にだけ競合他社が存在する。A社はコンピュータソフトの販売とコンサルティングを行っているのに対して，B社は販売だけを行っているかもしれない。

d 合併と買収が問題を複雑にするかもしれない。2020年度のある業界における平均年次売上高成長率が5％であったのに対して，2020年度のA社の売上高は20％成長したとしよう。素晴らしい業績のように見えるが，2020年度期首にA社は競合他社B社を買収しており，A社の売上高にB社の売上高が含まれていたらどうであろうか？A社の業績についての結論を出す前に，追加の分析が必要である。

e 異なる会計処理が採用されているかもしれない。同様の工場設備をA社は3年で減価償却しているのに対して，B社は5年で償却しているかもしれない。また，同

Also international comparisons can be difficult because of methods of accounting for similar items differing between countries.

f Information may not be available to calculate meaningful industry averages.

It may be possible to adjust for some of the above problems, but it makes the analysis more difficult to carry out, and also more dependent on assumptions and estimates, and thus less objective.

11.11 Balance sheet differences by business sector

The size of the numbers in a balance sheet varies by size of business. A single coffee shop with five employees would have a very small balance sheet size compared with a chain composed of hundreds of coffee shops, although the business activities might be similar. Where companies are of a similar size, there are also often very different balance sheets, based on the different business sector the companies operate in. Here, the **relative** size of the balance sheet items is being considered – so, for example, do fixed assets make up 10% of the company's assets, or are they 80%?

The following table compares balance sheet composition and size for four different business sectors, and makes some general comments.

Business	BS category	Size	Comment
Car maker	Land and buildings	Very large	Probably owns factories
	Plant and equipment	Very large	Factory machines
	Inventories	Large	Materials, WIP, completed cars
	Accounts payable	Large	Materials bought on credit
	Loans	Large	Needed to finance factories
Coffee shop	Land and buildings	Small / none	Probably rents premises
	Plant and equipment	Relatively large	Furniture and other equipment
	Inventories	Some, not large	Food/drink need replaced often
	Accounts receivable	Small	Not many credit sales
	Accounts payable	Not huge	Inventories bought on credit
Travel agent	Land and buildings	Small / none	Probably rents premises
	Plant and equipment	Relatively large	Furniture and office equipment
	Inventories	None	Not selling goods
Bank	Assets - loans given	Huge	Main business of most banks
	Liabilities - borrowing	Huge	Finance needed to give loans
	Inventories	None	Not selling goods

様の項目の会計処理が国によって異なる場合，国際比較も難しい。

f　有意な業界平均値の情報が入手できないかもしれない。

　以上の問題の一部は調整可能かもしれないが，分析が困難であったり，仮定や見積もりに依存し，結果として客観性を失うことになる。

11.11　業種による貸借対照表の異同

　貸借対照表の数値の大きさは企業規模によって変わる。従業員5人の一店舗だけのコーヒーショップは大規模チェーン店と比べると，事業活動は同様であるが，貸借対照表のサイズは小さい。同規模の会社の場合でも，業種の違いで貸借対照表は違ってくる。ここでは，貸借対照表の**相対的**サイズ－たとえば固定資産が資産の10％か，80％か－が考慮されている。

業種	BS 区分	大きさ	コメント
自動車メーカー	土地及び建物	非常に大きい	おそらく工場を所有
	機械装置及び備品	非常に大きい	工場の機械
	棚卸資産	大きい	原材料，仕掛品，完成品
	買掛金	大きい	材料を掛けで購入
	借入金	大きい	工場の調達資金
コーヒーショップ	土地及び建物	小さい／なし	おそらく店舗を賃借
	機械装置及び備品	比較的大きい	家具及びその他の設備
	棚卸資産	大きくない	フード／飲料，多くの場合，要交換
	売掛金	小さい	掛け売りは多くない
	買掛金	多額ではない	棚卸資産を掛けで購入
旅行代理店	土地及び建物	小さい／なし	おそらく店舗を賃借
	機械装置及び備品	比較的大きい	家具及び事務用備品
	棚卸資産	なし	商品なし
銀行	資産－貸出金	莫大	銀行の主たる業務
	負債－借入金	莫大	融資のための資金調達
	棚卸資産	なし	商品なし

However, even when operating in the same business sector, different companies' balance sheets could vary greatly due to different business methods. For example, one maker of mobile phones might own many factories, and thus have huge property, plant and equipment assets. Another might outsource nearly all phone production and so have a much smaller PPE total.

11.12 Income statement differences by business sector

As was seen in the case of the balance sheet, income statements too would differ depending on the business sector. Here are some simple examples.

Business	P&L category	Comparative Size	Comment
Car maker	Depreciation	Very large	Expensive fixed assets
	Cost of sales	Very large	Cost of materials, staff, energy
Coffee shop	Rent	Large	Premises usually rented
	Salaries and wages	Large	High proportion of costs
	Cost of sales	Not so large	High gross profit
Travel agent	Rent	Large	Premises usually rented
	Salaries and wages	Large	High proportion of costs
	Advertising	Large	Effective advertising needed
Bank	Interest received	Very large	From loans to customers
	Interest paid	Very large	From borrowings by bank

同じ業種でも，ビジネスのやり方の違いによって貸借対照表は異なる。たとえば自社の工場をもつ携帯電話メーカーと，製造を外注しているメーカーでは，前者の有形固定資産は巨額になるが，後者の有形固定資産はかなり小さくなる。

11.12　業種による損益計算書の異同

損益計算書も業種によって異なる。

業種	P&L 区分	相対的大きさ	コメント
自動車メーカー	減価償却費	非常に大きい	高額な固定資産
	売上原価	非常に大きい	材料費，労務費，経費
コーヒーショップ	賃借料	大きい	店舗は通常賃借
	給与及び賃金	大きい	高い原価率
	売上原価	あまり大きくない	高い粗利益率
旅行代理店	賃借料	大きい	店舗は通常賃借
	給与及び賃金	大きい	高い原価率
	広告費	大きい	効果的な広告が必要
銀行	受取利息	非常に大きい	顧客に対する融資より
	支払利息	非常に大きい	借入金より

12.1 Financial accounting and management accounting

Financial accounting focuses on providing financial information to **outsiders** to a business, such as shareholders, lenders, other creditors and tax authorities. The methods and reporting are **standardized, and in accordance with laws** and **regulations such as accounting standards.** The main purpose is to report on the **past,** in other words on events that have already happened. The financial accounting information is **public** and for **external** use.

Management (or **managerial**) accounting focuses on providing financial information to **insiders,** the **management** of a business, such as directors and managers. The methods and reporting are **not standardized,** and each business produces **what it considers useful and important.** Other key factors in the decision of what to prepare are the **time and resources** required to produce the information.

Although figures from the past are usually a key part of much management accounting, the purpose is to provide information to improve **future** decision-making and performance. The management accounting information is **confidential** and for **internal** use.

The Institute of Management Accountants is an international organization for people working in the field of management accounting. It has said management accounting "involves partnering in management decision making, devising planning and performance-management systems, and providing expertise in financial reporting and control to assist management in the formulation and implementation of an organization's strategy."

Management accounting increased in importance during the 19th century as businesses grew in size and complexity. Advances in information technology have made it possible to produce management accounting data which is much more detailed than in the past. It can also be produced much faster, so therefore is more useful as it is more recent. These are trends which will presumably continue.

12.2 Some common examples of management accounting activities

i **Budgets** are financial plans of income and expenditure over a certain period. Most companies would make one annually, some time before a new financial year starts. The

第12章 管理会計パート1

12.1 財務会計と管理会計

- 財務会計
  - 目的：財務会計は，株主，債権者および税務当局といった**企業外部の関係者**に対してすでに生起した**過去**の事象に関する財務情報を提供すること。
  - 特徴：記録方法と報告様式は**標準化されており，会計基準**をはじめとする各種制度や法規制に従う。財務会計情報は公表されるので公のものであり，**企業外部**で利用される。

- 管理会計
  - 目的：企業の**経営管理層**（部門管理者や経営者）などの**企業内部者**に対して，**将来**の意思決定と業績改善に必要な財務情報を提供すること。
  - 特徴：記録方法と報告様式は**標準化されておらず，**各事業にとって**有用で重要である情報**を作成する。重要となる要素は，情報作成に必要な時間と資源である。また，管理会計情報は**企業秘密**が多いので，**企業内部**で利用される。
  - 定義：「管理会計は，経営意思決定に活用され，計画策定と業績管理システムを構築し，そして，組織戦略の策定と実行において経営者を支援するために，財務報告と財務管理に専門性を提供するものである。」(IMA, 2008, p.1)
    - ✧ この定義は，管理会計領域で働く人々の国際組織である管理会計士協会（The Institute of Management Accountants: IMA）によるものである。
  - 管理会計の発展
    - ✧ 管理会計は，企業規模が拡大し，事業の複雑さが高まった19世紀を通じてその重要性を高めていった。今日におけるIT（情報技術）の進展は，従来よりも豊富で詳細な管理会計データを素早く提供することができるため，企業経営にとってますます有用なものになってきている。

12.2 管理会計の一般的な事例

i 予算
  - 特定の期間を通じた収益・費用に関する財務計画であり，毎年，新たな会計年

budget data is usually split into months or quarters, so that analysis using it can be carried on throughout the fiscal year it applies to. This is especially important for businesses which are **seasonal**, in other words have sales and/or costs which fluctuate depending on the time of year.

Example: An ice cream maker creates monthly budgets because there is a high seasonal variation in sales, with higher sales expected during the summer months. Using sales and cost of sales information from the same month in previous years would give more meaningful analysis than a monthly average.

Businesses need to be sure they have the appropriate resources, whether money, other assets or staff, to achieve their plans. A budget may predict problems with lack of resources, and allow action to be taken to add to them. Sometimes it may be necessary to revise the budget to be less ambitious to take into account the lack of resources.

The commonest kinds of budgets are profit and loss budgets, but balance sheet budgets are also sometimes created.

ii **Variance analysis**, which is done by comparing actual figures to budgets. Reports are created to aid the analysis of why actual figures achieved in reality (whether better or worse) differed from the budget. Like budgets themselves, this would also often be done on a monthly or quarterly basis. Such analysis can identify problems at an early stage, allowing action to be taken.

Variance analysis can also be used to evaluate the performance for subsidiaries, departments, products or people within a business.

iii **Cash flow forecasts,** which are carried out to make sure a business has enough cash to pay debts as they become due. Many businesses might do this monthly, but a business in severe financial difficulties might even have to do it daily.

Because it is attempting to predict when in time cash inflows and outflows will take place, a cash flow forecast does **not** use the accrual basis of accounting. So, for example, when payment will be received for sales on credit is key to a cash flow forecast, not when the sales took place. Similarly, depreciation is irrelevant, because it is not a flow of cash, but a calculation based on the matching principle.

度が始まる前に作成される。予算データは，通常，月次や四半期に区分される
ので，予算が適用される会計年度を通じて予算データを活用した分析が行われ
る。夏季や冬季など特定の期間に売上やコストが変動する**季節性**を有する事業
の場合，予算は特に重要である。

例：アイスクリーム販売業の月次予算。季節性の高い業種であるため，過去の同月の
売上高と売上原価情報を用いることが，月次平均売上高などを用いるよりも分析には
有用。

> 企業は，事業計画の達成のために必要な資源（資金や人材など）が適切にある
> かどうかを確認するために予算を策定する必要がある。予算が資源不足の問題
> を予測し，資源を追加するのに取るべき行動を可能にする。

> 一般的な予算は損益予算であるが，貸借対照表予算もしばしば作成される。

ii **予算差異分析**

> 予算差異分析は，予算の金額と実際の金額を比較してなされる。この分析は月
> 次または四半期ごとに行われるが，この差異（有利差異と不利差異）が生じた
> 理由を分析した報告書が作成される。

> 予算差異分析の結果の利用：

> ◇ 予算差異分析の結果から，企業は早期に問題を発見し，適切な行動をとる
> ことが可能となる。

> ◇ 予算差異分析の結果を用いて，部署や社員の業績評価に利用することもで
> きる。

iii **キャッシュ・フロー予測**（資金繰り予測）

> キャッシュ・フロー予測とは，企業が支払期日までに債務を支払うのに十分な
> 資金を有しているかどうか確認すること。財務状況が悪化しているような場合
> は，日々実施される必要がある。

> キャッシュ・フロー予測では，資金の流入と流出が見合うかどうかを予測する
> ことを企図しているため，発生主義会計は**適用されない**。

iv Producing **detailed income and cost information** on a company's products and services.

Example 1: A chain of coffee shops divides its sales information into coffee, tea, other drinks, hot food and cold food.

Example 2: A supermarket analyses sales by the amount sold per square meter of retail floor space in each of its shops.

Example 3: a chain of coffee shops might have a detailed breakdown of the cost for each different type of drink and food it sells, showing what the cost of the ingredients, staff time and utilities are. Clearly such information would often be combined with or produced with income analysis as in example 1 above. This would also allow the chain to try to especially increase sales of the more profitable products.

12.3 Decision making

How can and how should accounting and related numbers be used in decision making?

Example: a company is wondering whether to launch a new product or not. If it did, it estimates that over several years the income would be $ 9 million, variable costs $ 4 million and fixed costs $ 7 million. Should it launch the new product?

Answer: from this information alone, no. It would give a loss of $ 2 million.

This seems an easy decision, and it is clear how to use the numbers as an aid to making it. However, it is not always as clear as this. Also further information, not always purely numeric, could result in a different decision. Perhaps the company feels it needs to provide the product at a loss because it also provides other related products or services which are profitable. For example, mobile phones could be provided at a loss, if other services provided to customers were profitable enough.

12.4 Relevant costs

When making a monetary decision, only **relevant costs** should be included in the decision-making process. Two examples of costs which are not relevant are **sunk costs** and **unchangeable future costs**.

Sunk costs are costs already incurred which **cannot be recovered**.

Example 1: A person has a watch she no longer wants, and wishes to sell it. It originally cost $20. A friend has offered to pay $12 for the watch. In this situation, the $20 is a sunk cost and so should not be considered when making the decision.

Example 2: A company is considering whether to continue making gloves or not.

The additional revenue each year expected from sale of gloves is $8,000 and additional costs

iv　詳細な収益・費用情報

  ➢　製品・サービスに関する詳細な収益情報

　　例1：コーヒーチェーン店の場合

　　・コーヒー，紅茶，その他飲料，温かい食事および冷たい食事といった区分に
　　　分けて売上を管理する。

　　例2：スーパーマーケット

　　・各店舗の売場面積（㎡）ごとの売上高により売上分析を行う。

  ➢　製品・サービスに関する詳細な費用情報

　　例3：コーヒーチェーン店の場合

　　・材料費，人件費，水道光熱費などの費用を，販売している商品区分ごとにコ
　　　ストを把握して管理する。この情報は，上記の例1における収益分析と一緒
　　　に使用される。これにより，コーヒーチェーン店は，より収益性の高い製品
　　　の売上を増やすことに努めるであろう。

12.3　意思決定

　会計とそれに関連する数値はどのように経営意思決定に使用できるか，また，使用
すべきか？この問いに答えるために以下の例を挙げる。

例：ある企業では新製品を市場に投入するかどうか思案している。新製品を投入した
場合，数年間にわたって収益が$900万，変動費が$400万そして固定費が$700万もたら
されると見積もられている。新製品は投入されるべきか？

答え：これだけの情報であれば答えはノー。$200万の損失をもたらしうる。

　企業は常に上記の例のように意思決定支援に使うべき会計情報が明確なわけではな
い。また，数値化できないような情報があれば，意思決定は異なる。

例：新製品自体は損失を生み出してしまうが，当該製品が収益性の高い製品・サービ
スを生み出すなら，損失が生じても当該新製品を投入する意義はある。

12.4　関連原価

　お金に関する意思決定を行う際，意思決定プロセスには**関連原価**だけを含めるべき
である。関連しない原価の2つの代表例として，（1）**埋没原価**と（2）**変更不能将来
原価**がある。

ⅰ　埋没原価とは？

　埋没原価は，将来の特定の意思決定に影響を及ぼさない，過去に発生した原価であ
る。

例1：腕時計を所有しているある人が，それを売却したいとする。取得原価は$20であっ
たが，友人が$12での購入を申し出た。この場合，$20は埋没原価であり，意思決定に
使用すべきではない。

relating to making gloves are expected to be $6,000. The company owns a machine purchased for $10,000 to make gloves, which has no resale value, and no alternative use. What should the company's decision be?

Answer: The purchase price of the machine is a sunk cost and so should not be considered as part of the decision. Extra net income of $8,000 – $6,000 would be received, so the company should continue making gloves if there is no better alternative.

Unchangeable future costs are also **irrelevant** to a decision. Only future costs which can be changed as a result of the decision should be considered.

Example: consider again the situation of the new product launch decision. (Income $ 9 million, variable costs $ 4 million, fixed costs $ 7 million). Also, there is the additional information that included in the fixed cost estimate is $3 million of rent for a factory being rented at the moment. The rental contract cannot be shortened, and there is no other use for the factory. Should the business launch the new product or not?

Answer: the $ 3 million rent should not be considered in the decision, as it is not changeable. If rent is removed from consideration, it can be seen that launching the product would give additional net income of $ 1 million compared to not launching it.

$9 million (sales) – $ 4 million (variable costs) – $4 million (fixed costs except rent)

= $1 million extra income

Thus, if there is no better alternative, from this information, the product should be launched.

12.5 Fixed assets, depreciation and disposal of fixed assets

In financial accounting, the costs of fixed assets are spread over several periods using depreciation calculations. The financial accounting treatment of these amounts is usually **not appropriate** for decision making.

The original cost of a fixed asset already purchased is a sunk cost and so not relevant to a decision.

Depreciation (whether for one year or whether the accumulated depreciation on an asset) is simply an accounting calculation to allocate the original cost of an asset. It too is irrelevant to a decision.

If a decision involved disposing of a fixed asset, any inflows or outflows of money relating to the disposal **are relevant** to the decision.

Example: Company A, which has its own delivery van, is considering signing a four-year

例2：ある企業では，手袋の製造を続けるかどうか検討している。手袋の販売から期待される年間収益は$8,000であり，手袋製造のための追加原価は$6,000と見積もられている。同社は手袋の製造のために$10,000で購入した機械を所有しているが，すでに売却価値はゼロとなっており，他の用途への転用もできない。この場合，企業はどう意思決定すべきか？

答え：機械の購入代金は埋没原価であるので，意思決定の一部に含めるべきではない。追加収益$8,000 − $6,000が受け取られるので，同社はより良い代替案がない限り生産を続けるべきである。

ii　変更不能将来原価とは？

　変更不能将来原価は上記の埋没原価とともに，意思決定には**無関連**である。意思決定の結果変化する将来原価だけが考慮されるべきである。

例：上で取り上げた新製品の市場投入の例を考えよう（収益$900万，変動費$400万，固定費$700万）。追加情報として，固定費には，工場の家賃・地代が$300万含まれていることが分かった。賃貸契約では契約期間を短縮することはできず，工場以外にも使用することができない。この場合，同社は新製品を導入すべきか？

答え：$300万の家賃・地代は変更不可能なので，意思決定で考慮すべきではない。将来の家賃・地代を考慮しなければ，新製品は追加収益$100万をもたらす（以下の式参照）。よって新製品を導入すべきである。

$900万（売上高）− $400万（変動費）− $400万（家賃・地代を除く固定費）
　　　　　　　　　　　　= 追加収益$100万

12.5　有形固定資産，減価償却費および有形固定資産の処分

　有形固定資産の原価は減価償却を通じて，いくつかの会計期間に配分されるという財務会計上の処理は，意思決定では通常適切ではない。すでに購入した有形固定資産の取得原価は埋没原価なので，意思決定に**無関連**である。

　一方，有形固定資産の処分を含めて考えると，処分に伴う資金流入や流出は，意思決定と**関連性がある**。

例：配送用車両を所有するA社は，配送業務をアウトソーシングする4年契約の締結

contract to outsource its deliveries. Company A will have to pay the outsourcing company $2,250 each year for the next four years. Company A will annually save $2,000 on employing a driver and $500 on maintenance. The company van would not be needed and could be disposed of, for around $1,000 of disposal proceeds. The van originally cost $ 9,000 and has a net book value of $4,000. What decision should be made?

Answer: The original cost and accumulated depreciation on the van are not relevant costs and so the expected financial accounting loss on disposal of $4,000 – $1,000 = $3,000 is also not relevant. The disposal proceeds of $1,000, however, are relevant to the decision as that money will flow in.

Cost if outsourcing is done:

(4 × 2,250 per year) – 1,000 disposal proceeds = $8,000

Cost if current method continues:

4 × 2,500 per year (salary and maintenance) = $10,000

So if the decision is to be based purely on cost, the deliveries should be outsourced.

12.6 Opportunity cost

Opportunity cost is a term used from economics and means the income given up by choosing one option instead of another.

> **Opportunity cost = amount given up on best option**
> **– amount obtained by option chosen**

Example: If an investor invests in company A, he will receive a dividend of $600. If he invests in company B, he will receive a dividend of $200. Then the opportunity cost of investing in B is $600 – $200 = $400.

12.7 Fixed costs and variable costs

The operating profit of a business is its total sales revenue minus the expenses relating to its main business activities. Ignoring any non-operating income or expenses,

> **total profit = total sales revenue – total costs**

Costs can be divided into two types.

i Fixed costs. These are costs which are a fixed amount, which does not change even if the quantity of products made or sold do change.

Examples are the rent of an office, the fixed monthly salary of an office worker, or the cost of a new personal computer.

Fixed costs are often called **overheads**.

を検討している。アウトソーシングする場合，毎年$2,250をアウトソーシング会社に４年間支払う必要がある。これにより毎年，$2,000の運転手の給料と$500の車両維持費を節約できる。配送用車両を処分する場合，売却収入$1,000が得られる見込みである。車両の取得原価は$9,000，現在の帳簿価額は$4,000である。どのような意思決定がなされるべきか？

答え：車両の取得原価と減価償却累計額は無関連原価であるから，処分に係る財務会計上の損失「$4,000 − $1,000 = $3,000」は意思決定に無関連。売却収入の$1,000は，実際に資金が流入するので意思決定に関連する。

アウトソーシングが採用された場合のコスト：

$$（4年 \times \$2,250/年）－売却収入\$1,000 = \$8,000$$

現在の方式の採用を継続した場合のコスト：

$$4年 \times \$2,500/年（給料および維持費）= \$10,000$$

よって，もし意思決定が純粋に費用だけにもとづいておこなわれるのであれば，アウトソーシングするべきである。

12.6　機会原価

機会原価とは？

> 経済学の用語であり，あるオプションを選択することにより他のオプションによる所得を断念することを意味する。

> 機会原価＝最善のオプションにより断念した所得額 − 選択したオプションにより得られた所得額

例：ある投資家がA社に投資した場合，$600の配当金を受け取れる。B社に投資した場合は$200である。B社に投資した場合の機会原価は，$600 − $200 ＝ $400である。

12.7　固定費と変動費

営業利益は，以下のように計算することができる。

（営業）利益＝売上収益合計 −（本業に関する）費用合計

そして，費用は以下のように2種類に分けることができる。

i　**固定費**

> 製品の生産量や販売量の変化に関係なく，一定額発生するコスト。大半は間接費である（固定費発生の特徴は，13.3節を参照のこと）。

> 例：事務所の家賃，事務系社員の月給，減価償却費など。

ii Variable costs. These are costs whose total amount does change, increasing or decreasing with the level of production or sales.

Examples are hourly wages paid to factory staff, bonuses paid to sales staff, costs of transporting goods to customers, the cost of materials used in production, or the cost of buying goods for re-sale.

It is more accurate to say that fixed costs do not change over a certain **relevant range**. For example, the rent of an office with a maximum capacity of 50 people would be considered as a fixed cost, provided that the number of staff is 50 or fewer. However, if growth in the business meant that more than 50 staff needed to be employed, a larger office, or one more office, would be needed.

Whereas normally fixed costs are usually considered as a total, often variable costs per unit are key to analysis. Here, **unit** means one – so one tonne of steel or one car, for example.

12.8 The basic profit formula

Consider a business making one product, which generates a total profit, P. The business **produces and sells** a certain quantity (Q) of the product. The business has two kinds of costs, total fixed costs (FC) and variable costs per unit (VC). The product is sold at a certain sales price per unit, SP.

A formula linking all these can be built up as follows.

total profit (P) = total sales revenue – total costs

and also:

i total sales revenue = quantity × sales price per unit = Q × SP
ii total costs = total fixed costs + total variable costs
= total fixed costs + (quantity × variable cost per unit)
= FC + (Q × VC)

Combining these the formula can be rewritten as

P = (Q × SP) – FC – (Q × VC) and using basic algebra we have
P = Q × (SP – VC) – FC but in fact as will be seen it is often useful to write the formula as:
P + FC = Q × (SP – VC)

Note carefully that P and FC are referring to **total** profit and **total** fixed costs, whereas SP (sales

ii 変動費

> 生産量や販売量の増減に応じて発生額が変化するコスト（変動費発生の特徴は，13.2節参照のこと）。

> 例：時給制の工場作業員，販売員に支払う特別報酬（ボーナス），顧客への製品の輸送費，原材料費，仕入商品の売上原価など。

現実には，上記の通り完全に固定費または変動費に区分できないコストも存在する。固定費は，ある特定の範囲内でのみ変化しないと言った方が正確である。例えば，50人収容可能な事務所の家賃は固定費であるが，従業員が50人を超過すると新たな事務所が必要となるため，ある一定水準から固定費は増額される。これを準固定費という。

通常固定費は合計額で考えられるが，分析ではしばしば単位当たり変動費がカギとなる。ここで単位は1つのことであり，例えば，1トンの鉄や1台の車などである。

12.8　利益計算の基本公式

想定例：以下のケースを想定した場合の利益計算の公式を考える。

> ある企業では，単一の製品をある量（Q）だけ生産・販売し，利益総額Pを生み出している。同社のコストは，総固定費（FC）と単位当たり変動費（VC）の2種類である。製品は，単位当たり販売価格（SP）で販売される。

利益計算の公式

利益総額（P）＝総売上収益－総費用
総売上収益＝生産・販売量×単位当たり販売価格＝$Q \times SP$
総費用＝総固定費＋総変動費
　　　＝総固定費＋（生産・販売量×単位当たり変動費）
　　　＝$FC +（Q \times VC）$

上記の式を統合すると以下のように書き換えられる。

$$P =（Q \times SP）- FC -（Q \times VC）$$
$$P = Q \times（SP - VX）- FC$$
$$P + FC = Q \times（SP - VC）$$

※PとFCは利益**総額**と**総**固定費を意味するのに対し，SP（販売価格）とVC（変動費）は**製品1単位当たり**の情報を意味する点に注意されたい。なお，単純化のため量（Q）は生産量と販売量の両方を意味するので未販売の在庫はないものとする。

price) and VC (variable cost) are information about a **unit** of the product.

For simplicity, it is assumed that the quantity Q refers both to the amount produced and to the amount sold, so there is no unsold inventory.

This formula can also be used for a business buying a product for re-sale, rather than making it itself.

The formula can be used to make calculations, and hence to aid decisions relating to profit, fixed and variable costs, quantities to produce and/or sell, and price, provided only one term of the formula is unknown.

12.9 The formula in profit calculations and decisions

Example: A company is going to make and sell 200 toy boats with a sales price of $10, total fixed costs of $1,000 and a variable cost per unit of $4. How much will its profit be?

Answer: $P = Q \times (SP - VC) - FC$

$= 200 \times (10 - 4) - 1,000 = \$200$ profit

Example: A company is going to make and sell 1,000 baseball bats with a sales price of $10 and a variable cost per unit of $6. It is aiming to make a profit of at least $1,800. What is the maximum its fixed costs can be to achieve this target?

Answer: Assume the minimum desired profit, $1,800, is achieved and set P = $1,800.

$P + FC = Q \times (SP - VC)$ so $FC = Q \times (SP - VC) - P$

$FC = 1,000 \times (10 - 6) - 1,800 = 4,000 - 1,800 = \$2,200$

So provided fixed costs do not rise over $2,200, the company can achieve its aim.

Often a business is trying to find out what quantity, or price, or fixed costs, or variable cost per unit will allow it to have a profit (or loss) of zero, in other words, what levels are needed to **break even.** This means that profit = 0, and so the formula simplifies to

$$FC = Q \times (SP - VC)$$

Example: A company wants to know what sales price it needs to charge to break even if fixed costs are $20,000, the sales quantity is expected to be 500 and variable costs per unit are $12.

Answer: $FC = Q \times (SP - VC)$ so $(FC \div Q) = SP - VC$

and so $SP = (FC \div Q) + VC = (20,000 \div 500) + 12 = \$52$

It can be verified that this is the correct answer by using the formula with all the numbers as follows:

12.9 利益計算公式と意思決定

　上記の利益計算の公式は，以下の例に示したように1つの変数が未知の場合に適用され，企業のさまざまな意思決定に活用される。

例：ある企業が，販売価格1艘\$10，総固定費\$1,000および製品1単位当たり変動費\$4で，200艘のおもちゃのボートを生産販売している。利益はいくらになるか？
答え：

$$P = Q \times (SP - VC) - FC$$
$$= 200艘 \times (\$10 - \$4) - \$1,000 = \$200 （利益額）$$

例：ある企業が，販売価格1本\$10および製品1単位当たり変動費\$6で，1,000本の野球バットを生産販売する予定である。そして少なくとも\$1,800の利益の達成が目標としている。当該利益目標を達成できる固定費の許容額はいくらか？
答え：

　最低目標利益額\$1,800を達成することが想定されているので，$P = \$1,800$ とする。
$$P + FC = Q \times (SP - VC) であるから FC = Q \times (SP - VC) - P$$
$$FC = 1,000本 \times (\$10 - \$6) - \$1,800 = \$4,000 - \$1,800 = \$2,200$$
　したがって，固定費が\$2,200を超過しなければ目標利益を達成できる。
・　損益分岐点とは
　➤　利益（または損失）がゼロになる生産量（販売量）。以下の式により計算される。

$$FC = Q \times (SP - VC)$$

例：ある企業では，固定費が\$20,000，予測販売量が500，そして単位当たり変動費が\$12の場合に，損益分岐点を超えるのに必要な販売価格を知りたいと思っている。
答え：$FC = Q \times (SP - VC)$ であるから $(FC \div Q) = SP - VC$
　　したがって，$SP = (FC \div Q) + VC = (\$20,000 \div 500) + \$12 = \$52$
　　以下のように公式を適用して正解を検証できる。

$P = Q \times (SP - VC) - FC = 500 \times (52 - 12) - 20,000 = 0$, zero profit or loss

12.10 Contribution margin

A phrase often used with the formula is **contribution margin**, which is the difference between sales price and variable costs.

So **total contribution margin = Q × (SP – VC)** and

contribution margin per unit = SP – VC

The contribution margin per unit is showing how much each extra unit contributes to **covering the fixed costs (overheads)**.

Question: A company makes a product with a unit contribution margin of 100. It has fixed costs of 2,000. What quantity is required to be produced to cover the fixed costs?

Answer: This question can be restated to "what quantity must be produced to break even if fixed costs are 2,000?"

$P + FC = Q \times (SP - VC)$

$0 + 2,000 = Q \times 100$

$Q = 2,000 \div 100 = 20$ units

So this kind of question can be answered quickly from the formula:

Q needed to cover FC = FC ÷ contribution margin per unit

Note that it is possible for a company to make one or many different products, all with positive contribution margins, but still make overall losses, because the total contribution margin is not high enough to cover fixed costs.

Note also that a positive contribution margin per unit implies that each extra unit gives the company higher net revenue, so as many units as can be sold should be produced **unless there is another product with a higher contribution whose production could be increased instead**.

$$P = Q \times (SP - VC) - FC = 500 \times (\$52 - \$12) - \$20{,}000 = 0 \quad (\text{損益ゼロ})$$

12.10 　貢献利益

貢献利益とは？

➢ 販売価格と変動費の差額。以下の関係が成り立つ。

貢献利益総額 ＝ Q × (SP − VC)
製品1単位当たり貢献利益 ＝ SP − VC

この式は，各製品1単位が，**固定費を回収する**のにどれだけ貢献するかということを表している。

例：ある企業では，製品1単位当たり貢献利益が100の製品を生産している。固定費が2,000であるとき，固定費を回収するのに必要な生産量（販売量）いくらか？

答え：上記の問題文は「固定費が2,000であるとき，損益分岐点の生産量はいくらか？」と書き換えることができる。

$$P + FC = Q \times (SP - VC)$$
$$0 + 2{,}000 = Q \times 100$$
$$Q = \frac{2{,}000}{100} = 20 \text{単位}$$

したがって，この種の問題は以下の公式を使うとすぐに回答できる。

$$FC \text{の回収に必要な} Q = \frac{FC}{1\text{単位当たり貢献利益}}$$

ただし，企業は単一または複数の種類の製品をすべて正の貢献利益で生産することは可能であるが，依然として全体では損失となることがある。なぜなら，貢献利益の合計額が固定費を回収するのに十分ではないからである。

また，正の単位当たり貢献利益は，企業により高い収益をもたらすことを意味するので，**より高い貢献利益をもたらすような他の製品が増産されない限り**，販売可能な量だけ製品が生産されるべきである。

13.1 Graphical representations of revenue, costs and quantity

It can be helpful to visualize the structure and relationship of revenue, costs and quantity by using graphs.

13.2 Graphs of variable costs

If nothing is produced, no variable costs are incurred. Starting from (0,0) the graph of **total variable costs** rises in a straight line, as each extra unit produced adds the same amount to total variable costs.

The graph of **variable costs per unit** shows that, regardless of the quantity produced, the variable cost is the same. This could represent, for example, the cost of the coffee in a cup of coffee, or the electricity cost per hour of running a machine in a factory.

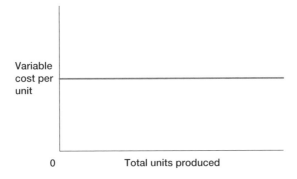

第**13**章　管理会計パート2

第13章

13.1　収益，費用および量のグラフ表示

収益，費用および生産量や販売量の構造と関係を視覚化することは有益である。

13.2　変動費のグラフ

何も生産されなければ変動費は発生しない。追加の製品単位は同額の変動費を発生させるので，**総変動費**（変動費線）は，（0.0）から始まり比例的に上昇する。

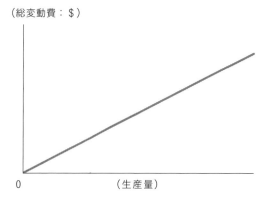

（総変動費：＄）

0　　　　　　（生産量）

製品単位当たり変動費は，生産量に関係なく，変動費が一定であることを示している。

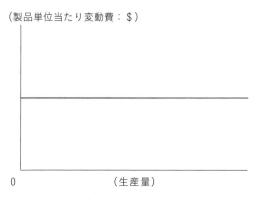

（製品単位当たり変動費：＄）

0　　　　　　（生産量）

13.3 Graphs of fixed costs

The graph of **total fixed costs** shows that, whether production is zero or higher, the amount remains the same.

The graph of **fixed costs per unit** shows that as production increases, the fixed cost per unit falls.

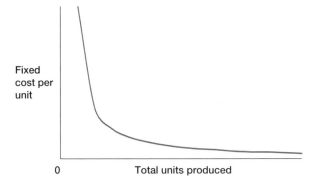

13.4 Graphs of total costs and total revenue

A graph of **total costs**, so **total fixed costs plus total variable costs**, would look like the following graph. There will be the full level of fixed costs even when production is zero, then the cost line would rise in a straight line as the same extra variable cost is added for each extra unit.

13.3　固定費のグラフ

　総固定費のグラフは，生産量がゼロかそれ以上ならば同額のまま推移することを示している。

（総固定費：$）

0　　　　　　　　（生産量）

　製品単位当たり固定費のグラフは，生産量が増大するにつれて製品単位当たり固定費が減少していくことを示している。

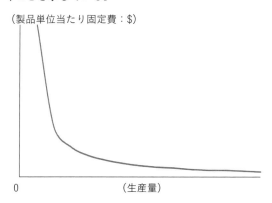

（製品単位当たり固定費：$）

0　　　　　　　　（生産量）

13.4　総費用・総収益のグラフ

　総固定費と総変動費を足した総費用のグラフは，以下のような形をとる。生産量がゼロの時でも固定費があるので，総費用線は，そこから追加の生産量に対して同額の追加の変動費が線形に上昇する形になっている。

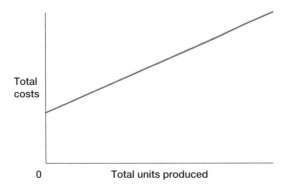

Total costs

0   Total units produced

The **total revenue** graph below is similar to the one for total variable costs, in that the revenue from zero units is zero, and so the graph commences from (0,0). It also rises in a straight line as for each extra unit, the extra revenue is the same.

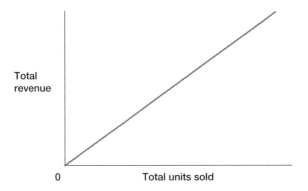

Total revenue

0   Total units sold

13.5 Break-even point shown graphically

The graphs of total revenue and costs could be drawn together as below.

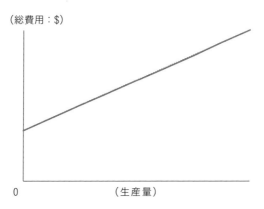

（総費用：$）

0   （生産量）

　以下の総収益のグラフは総変動費のグラフと類似しており，生産量がゼロのときは収益もゼロとなり，（0,0）から増加していく。追加の生産量に対して比例的に増加していき，追加の収益もまた同じである。

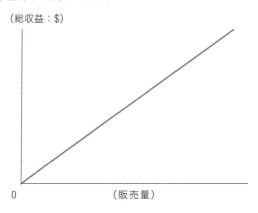

（総収益：$）

0   （販売量）

13.5　損益分岐点のグラフ表示

　総収益と総費用のグラフを1つに合わせると以下のようになる。

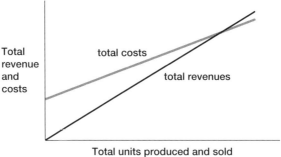

Total revenue and costs

total costs

total revenues

Total units produced and sold

The point where the total revenue line meets the total cost line is the level of production giving a break-even result. Below the break-even point, the gap between the two lines shows the loss at that level of production. Above the break-even point, the gap represents the profit. The graph shows clearly why higher levels of production should lead to higher profits for products with a positive contribution margin.

13.6 Mixed costs

Costs which are neither perfectly fixed nor variable are often called mixed costs. They can often be split into a fixed part and a variable part. A graph of such costs would look like the total cost graph above. This is because – just as in the combination of total fixed and variable costs – such a mixed cost is not zero even at a level of production of zero.

An example could be a factory's electricity bill, where at a level of production of zero, there is still a certain amount of electricity used to heat and light the offices used by staff not working to directly produce goods.

13.7 Fixed costs and relevant range

As mentioned earlier, in reality many fixed costs are only fixed over a certain relevant range. So, for example, renting one production facility may be enough for a business making 4,000 units of product, but two such shops may be needed if more than 4,000 are made, and three if more than 8,000 are made. A graph similar to the one below could represent this. This shows how a small increase in production could lead to a large increase in fixed costs if a relevant range boundary is crossed.

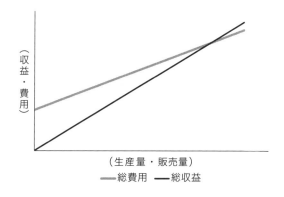

（収益・費用）

（生産量・販売量）

━━ 総費用　━━ 総収益

　総収益線と総費用線の交点が，損益が分岐する生産水準を表す。損益分岐点以下の生産水準では損失が発生し，同点を上回っていれば利益が生ずることを示している。この図から，より高い生産水準がなぜ高水準の利益をもたらすかを明らかにしている。

13.6　準変動費

準変動費とは？
- ➤ 完全に固定費でも変動費でもない費用であり，固定費部分と変動費部分に分けられる。
- ➤ このグラフは総費用のグラフ（13.4節参照）とほぼ同一となる。
- ➤ 例：工場の電力料（生産量がゼロの時でも生産部門に関わっていない部門における電力消費があるため）

13.7　一定の範囲を有する固定費：準固定費

　固定費は，現実にはある一定の範囲内で固定されていると考えられる。例えば，4,000単位の生産には現在借り受けている工場設備で十分だが，さらに4,000単位の生産が必要になると倍の工場設備が必要になる。8,000単位を超えれば3倍必要である。こうした準固定費をグラフ化すると以下のように示すことができる。
　この図はほんのわずかな生産量の増加が，固定費の大幅な増加を招くことを示している。

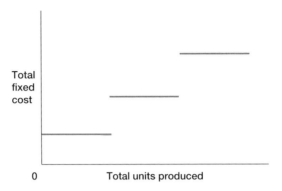

Total fixed cost

0   Total units produced

13.8 Two unknown terms in the basic profit equation

If information for two formulas is provided, then they can be solved for two unknown terms, using the mathematical method of simultaneous equations.

Question: Company A and company B sell the same product for the same price. Company A has fixed costs of $100 and variable costs of $10 per unit. Company B has fixed costs of $200 and variable costs of $8. What is the unit sales price at which these companies will have the same break-even point?

Answer: The question is about unit sales price, but neither SP nor Q are known.
It is a break-even question so use $FC = Q \times (SP - VC)$.

For A: $100 = Q \times (SP - 10)$ For B: $200 = Q \times (SP - 8)$
Subtracting A from B on both sides:
$200 - 100 = (Q \times SP) - 8Q - (Q \times SP) + 10 Q$, giving $100 = 2Q$ and so $Q = 50$
Using $Q = 50$ in either A or B's formula will give $SP = 12$.
So both companies will break even if their unit sales price is $12, and that will take place when quantity is 50.

13.9 Fixed costs, variable costs and profitability

A publishing company is considering two business methods.
Method 1: printing books itself and selling them.
The company finds it can rent a combined workshop and warehouse for a total of $6,000 a year and lease printing machinery for $4,000, so total fixed costs are $10,000. On average the unit materials and labor costs to produce a book are $2.

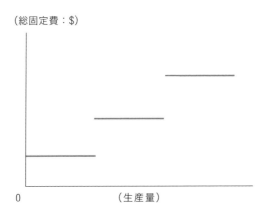

（総固定費：$）

0   （生産量）

13.8　利益計算公式に2つの未知の変数がある場合

　もし2つの公式がある場合，連立方程式を解けば2つの未知の変数が判明する。

例：A社とB社は同じ場所で同一の製品を販売している。A社の固定費は$100，単位当たり変動費は$10であるのに対し，B社の固定費は$200，単位当たり変動費は$8である。A社とB社がともに同一の損益分岐点を有するときの単位当たり販売価格（販売単価）はいくらか？

答え：この問題は，単位当たり販売価格（販売単価）についてであるが，SPとQの両方が未知である。損益分岐点に関わる問題なので，$FC = Q \times (SP - VC)$ の公式を用いる。

　A社について：$100 = Q \times (SP - 10)$　　　B社について：$200 = Q \times (SP - 8)$
　B社の式からA社を差し引くと：

$$200 - 100 = (Q \times SP) - 8Q - (Q \times SP) + 10Q$$
$$\text{この式を展開すると，} 100 = 2Q \text{であるから} Q = 50$$
$$Q = 50 \text{をA社とB社の公式に代入すれば} SP = 12$$

したがって，両社とも販売単価が$12のときに損益分岐点となり，販売量は50となる。

13.9　固定費，変動費および収益性

　想定ケース：ある出版社では以下の2つの代替案を検討している。

➢　代替案1：自社で本を印刷し販売する。

　　◇　諸条件：

　　　　・　固定費（$10,000／年）：作業場兼倉庫の家賃（$6,000／年），印刷機のリース料（$4,000／年）

Method 2: outsourcing the printing of the books.

The unit price payable to the outsourcing company is on average $6 a book. A warehouse will be needed, costing $2,000 a year in rent, the only fixed costs.

A decision has to be made between:

Method 1: higher fixed costs and lower variable costs per unit

Method 2: lower fixed costs and higher variable costs per unit

Assume that whether the books are printed in-house or outsourced, the selling price is unchanged. What could be done to help the publishing company make a decision which maximizes its profits?

Use the fact that total costs = total fixed costs + total variable costs

$$= FC + (Q \times VC)$$

Method 1: total costs = $10,000 + (Q \times 2)$

Method 2: total costs = $2,000 + (Q \times 6)$

What quantity of books produced would mean that total costs were equal?

$10,000 + 2Q = 2,000 + 6Q$ which gives $4Q = 8,000$ and so Q is 2,000.

The advice that could be given to the publishing company is that if a quantity of 2,000 is sold, costs will be the same. Below 2,000 books, Method 2 will result in lower costs and therefore higher profits. Above 2,000 books, Method 1 will result in lower costs and therefore higher profits.

If the books could be sold on average for $10, then profitability would be as follows for various quantities.

Quantity	income	method 1		method 2		difference
		costs	profit/loss	costs	profit/loss	
0	0	10,000	− 10,000	2,000	− 2,000	− 8,000
500	5,000	11,000	− 6,000	5,000	0	− 6,000
1,000	10,000	12,000	− 2,000	8,000	2,000	− 4,000
1,250	12,500	12,500	0	9,500	3,000	− 3,000
2,000	20,000	14,000	6,000	14,000	6,000	0
3,000	30,000	16,000	14,000	20,000	10,000	4,000
20,000	200,000	50,000	150,000	122,000	78,000	72,000

- ・ 1冊の本の単位当たり変動費：$2の原材料費と労務費
- ➤ 代替案2：本の印刷をアウトソーシングする。
  - ◆ 諸条件：
    - ・ 1冊の本の単位当たり変動費：1冊当たり$6
    - ・ 固定費：倉庫の家賃（$2,000／年）

各代替案の費用構造の特徴
- ➤ 代替案1：より高い固定費とより低い単位当たり変動費
- ➤ 代替案2：より低い固定費とより高い単位当たり変動費

代替案選択のための意思決定のための計算（前提：いずれの代替案を選択しても販売価格は変化しない）

$$総費用 = 総固定費 + 総変動費 = FC + (Q \times VC)$$
$$代替案1：総費用 = \$10,000 + (Q \times \$2)$$
$$代替案2：総費用 = \$2,000 + (Q \times \$6)$$

何冊の本を生産するかということは，両代替案の費用合計額が等しいことを意味するので，

$$\$10,000 + \$2Q = \$2,000 + \$6Q$$
$$\$4Q = \$8,000であるからQ = 2,000冊$$

したがって，2,000冊販売されるのであればいずれの代替案を選択しても同じだが，2,000冊を境に以下の違いが生まれる。
- ➤ 2,000冊超：代替案1を選択
- ➤ 2,000冊未満：代替案2を選択

本が平均して$10／冊で販売できる場合，販売部数に対する収益性は以下のように示すことができる。

販売量 (冊)	収益 ($)	代替案1		代替案2		差額 ($)
		費用 ($)	損益 ($)	費用 ($)	損益 ($)	
0	0	10,000	− 10,000	2,000	− 2,000	− 8,000
500	5,000	11,000	− 6,000	5,000	0	− 6,000
1,000	10,000	12,000	− 2,000	8,000	2,000	− 4,000
1,250	12,500	12,500	0	9,500	3,000	− 3,000
2,000	20,000	14,000	6,000	14,000	6,000	0
3,000	30,000	16,000	14,000	20,000	10,000	4,000
20,000	200,000	50,000	150,000	122,000	78,000	72,000

From this it can be seen:

i Lower fixed costs give a lower risk of large losses when quantity is low

ii Lower fixed costs give a lower break-even quantity

iii Lower variable costs give much higher profit when quantity is high, and this can become very high indeed.

It can be seen from the above example, and from the Basic Equation itself that profits increase as quantity goes up, provided products are making a positive marginal contribution. This is a major reason companies wish to expand in size.

13.10 Mergers and acquisitions

A merger is when two businesses merge together, and an acquisition is when one business buys another. The phrase mergers and acquisitions, often abbreviated to M&A, is used to describe such various business **combinations**.

Companies engage in mergers and acquisitions for various reasons, such as a desire to grow quickly in size, or to obtain technology or customers. One reason relating to fixed costs is the hope that a business combination could reduce them in total.

For example, if two banks from the same country merged, they may well have branches which are very near each other, and so some could be closed. Or it may be that company X has forty internal accounting staff, and company Y has twenty, but actually fifty will be enough to do the combined company's accounting work if X acquires Y.

There could also be effects on variable costs. For example, if company C orders 10,000 tonnes of steel a year to use in its products, and company D orders 5,000 tonnes, it may be that a combined company ordering 15,000 tonnes a year could negotiate with suppliers to obtain a lower price per tonne.

Example: Company A wants to increase the size of its business, and is considering acquiring a smaller rival making similar products, company B. Because an acquisition is a risky transaction, A decides that the acquisition should only be done if within one year A can recover all the extra costs relating to the acquisition, without assuming any increase in the sales of either company after the businesses are combined. The following current information about the two companies is available.

以上の検討から以下のことが指摘できる。

➢ 固定費を低くすると，販売量が少ないときの巨額の損失を惹起するリスクを低減する。
➢ 固定費を低くすると，損益分岐点販売量が低い水準で維持できる。
➢ 変動費を低くすると，販売量が大きいときにより高い利益をもたらす。

販売規模の拡大：販売量が増えるにつれて利益が増大するので，販売された製品は正の限界利益（貢献利益）をもたらす。これが，企業が規模を拡大したい主な理由である。

13.10　合併・買収

合併・買収（M&A）：合併は2つの企業が一つになること，また，買収は，ある企業が他の企業（事業）を買い取ることを意味する。M&Aは総称して**企業結合**と呼ばれる。企業は迅速な企業規模の拡大や技術や顧客の獲得などさまざまな理由でM&Aを行うが，特に固定費に関する理由として，企業結合による固定費の減少を期待することがあげられる。

➢ 例1（固定費の削減）：2つの国内銀行の合併に伴い近隣の支店を統合したり，合併により経理などの管理部門の社員数を削減することができる。
➢ 例2（変動費の削減）：C社が10,000トン，D社が5,000トンの鉄を原材料として発注している場合，両社が合併した後は，15,000トンをサプライヤーに発注することになるため，1トン当たりの仕入価格を低減するように交渉できる。

例：A社は事業規模拡大のため，同社よりも小規模な競合他社のB社の買収を検討している。買収にはリスクを伴うので，A社は，企業結合後の売上増加を見込まず，自社の買収に関連する超過コスト全額を1年以内に回収することができるかどうかを判断基準とした。両社の情報は以下の通りである。

Current situation	Company A	Company B
Fixed costs	18,000	25,000
Total sales	120,000	70,000
Variable costs per unit	15	12
Annual quantity of sales	6,000	4,000

Company A also makes various cost estimates in the event of an acquisition as follows.

i After acquisition both companies will be able to reduce their variable cost per unit by $1 on average, due to greater efficiency.

ii A total of $ 8,000 savings on fixed costs can be achieved for the combined businesses.

iii The total costs of acquisition payable by company A – closing an office, terminating some staff, reorganizing the businesses, fees payable to accountants and lawyers – are estimated to be $21,000.

Should company A go ahead with the acquisition?

Answer: The question can be rewritten as: will the combined business make at least $21,000 more profit within one year than the current situation, which is A operating alone?

The **current** profits of A, from the basic equation can be calculated as follows.

$$P (A) = Q \times (SP - VC) + FC = (Q \times SP) - (Q \times VC) - FC$$
$$= 120,000 - (6,000 \times 15) - 18,000 = 12,000$$

This currently earned 12,000 must be compared with the profits after the acquisition.

The **current** profits of B, from the basic equation can be calculated as follows.

$$P (B) = (Q \times SP) - (Q \times VC) - FC$$
$$70,000 - (4,000 \times 12) - 25,000 = -3,000$$

Actually, as P is negative, B currently has **losses** of 3,000, but that is **not** a key point, because A does not own B **now**. A is interested in B's future performance, as part of a business combination with A. A table to aid with decision-making can be constructed as follows, assuming a combination took place.

現在の状況	A社	B社
固定費（$）	18,000	25,000
売上高（$）	120,000	70,000
単位当たり変動費（$）	15	12
年間販売量（t）	6,000	4,000

A社が見積もっている買収にかかわるさまざまな費用。

ⅰ．買収後に効率性を向上させることで，平均$1の単位当たり変動費が削減可能。

ⅱ．企業結合により$8,000の固定費を削減可能。

ⅲ．A社が支払うべき取得費用（事務所の閉鎖，人員削減，ビジネス再構築，会計士と弁護士への報酬）は$21,000。

A社はこの買収を遂行すべきか。

答え：上記の問題は「企業結合により，A社が単独で事業を行っている現在の状況よりも，少なくとも$21,000多い利益を生み出すであろうか」と書き換えられる。

A社の現在の利益は，利益の基本公式から以下のように計算できる。

$$P(A) = Q \times (SP - VC) + FC = (Q \times SP) - (Q \times VC) - FC$$
$$= \$120,000 - (6,000t \times \$15) - \$18,000 = \$12,000$$

この$12,000の利益を，取得後の利益と比較。

B社の現在の利益は，基本公式から以下のように計算できる。

$$P(B) = (Q \times SP) - (Q \times VC) - FC$$
$$= \$70,000 - (4,000t \times \$12) - \$25,000 = -\$3,000$$

実際にB社は現在$3,000の**損失**を発生させているが，まだA社はB社を所有していないから**問題ではない**。A社はB社の将来の業績に関心を有しているおり，企業結合が行われた場合の意思決定を支援する表を以下のように作成できる。

A's current profit	12,000	
B's current loss	− 3,000	
A's variable cost savings	6,000	6,000 × $1
B's variable cost savings	4,000	4,000 × $1
Total fixed cost savings	8,000	for combined business
Profit before acquisition costs	27,000	
Acquisition costs	− 21,000	
Total profits	6,000	for combination of A and B

From these numbers, A should go ahead with the acquisition of B, as the condition of recovering at least all acquisition costs within a year has been met, and in fact there are further profits of $6,000.

This shows that with sufficient savings from fixed and variable costs, the acquisition of even a loss-making company could generate increased profits in future.

（単位: US$）

A社の現在の利益	12,000	
B社の現在の損失	−3,000	
A社の変動費節約額	6,000	6,000 × $1
B社の変動費節約額	4,000	4,000 × $1
総固定費節約額	8,000	事業統合による節約額
取得費控除前利益	27,000	
取得費	−21,000	
利益合計額	6,000	A社とB社の企業結合による利益

結論：上記の表から，1年以内に取得費用の少なくとも全額が回収でき，実際の将来$6,000をもたらすので，A社はB社の取得を進めるべきである。このことは，変動費と固定費の削減を通じて，たとえ損失を計上する企業の取得であっても利益がもたらしうることを示している。

Questions (Solutions at www.stuart-brison.com)

Question 2-1

A company has current assets of $14,000, liabilities of $16,000 and equity of $1,500. What is the value of its non-current assets?

Question 2-2

Create a balance sheet from the following information in dollars, for the company ABC Limited as of 30 September 2019.

Office equipment 3,300   Patent 400   Share capital 100

Bank account 2,600   Inventory 150   Accounts payable 550

Retained earnings 2,700   Accounts receivable 1,200

Corporation tax liability 1,000   Bank loan 3,300

Both the bank loan and the tax liability fall due within a year.

Question 3-1

Which element of accounting are each of the following an example of?

i)   An amount of $12,000 paid for advertising in a newspaper

ii) $10,000 lent by a company to an employee for three months

iii)   A bonus paid to an employee

iv)   A valuable painting bought for $100,000 used to decorate the office

v)   A penalty of $150 paid to the tax authorities because the company was late in submitting its tax return

vi)   A fee paid to a recruitment companyfor introducing a staff member

vii) The right to use a certain brand name, bought for $100,000

viii) $25,000 paid as compensation to an employee who was injured due to a safety problem in the company's factory

Question 3-2

Prepare an income statement for FGH Limited for the year ending 31 March 2019 from the following information in thousands of dollars.

Sales	12,000	Cost of sales	9,800
Wages and salaries	330	Rent	185
Insurance	64	Depreciation	225
Interest received	17	Advertising	188
Corporation tax expense	120		
Loss on disposal of fixed asset	88		

Question 4-1

A company sells three products. Complete the following table:

Product	Sales	Cost of sales	Gross profit
A	1,000	850	?
B	2,200	?	100
C	?	500	80
Totals	?	?	?

Question 4-2

This is inventory information about a company with a fiscal year which is the calendar year.It buys and sells steel, and sold 100 tons during the year.

Steel inventory		tons	price per ton ($)
Opening	January 1st	40	11.5
Purchases	June	50	10
Purchases	October	30	8

Calculate the value of closing inventory and cost of sales using:

i FIFO ii Weighted average, with one calculation per year

Which would give a higher profit for the fiscal year?

Question 5-1

A company is given a choice when buying a machine for its factory, either to buy on one month's credit for $10,000, or to pay cash, in which case a discount will be given and the price will be $9,500. In the seller's catalogue, the machine price is listed as $10,000.

The company chose to pay cash. Delivering the machine cost $500, and setting it up ready for use cost $1,000. The raw materials the machine will use in its first month were also bought for cash for $800. What is the initial cost of the machine?

Question 5-2

i A company buys a van for $17,000. It assumes a useful life of five years and residual value of $1,000. The van is bought on 7 January 2019. The company's financial year ends each 30 September. Show the expected fixed asset net book value in the balance sheet and depreciation numbers in the profit and loss account for each of the financial years 2019 to 2024 inclusive. Use the straight line method.

ii if the van was actually sold on 26 June 2021 for $3,000, what would the profit or loss on disposal be?

Question 6-1

A company has the following balance sheet information.

	Assets	Liabilities	Share Capital
FY 2018	1,200	800	50
FY 2019	1,400	1,100	50

What can be said about its results during FY 2019?

Question 6-2

i   A company has the following retained earnings figures.

FY 2019: $26,300   FY 2020: $ 27,100

What was its profit or loss for FY 2020?

ii   A company has the following net asset figures.

FY 2019: $121,000   FY 2020: $ 147,000

What was its profit or loss for FY 2020, if it also increased share capital in FY 2019 by $ 3,000 and in FY 2020 by $ 5,000?

iii   A company has assets of $12,000 and liabilities of $2,000 at the end of FY 2018. Two years later at the end of FY 2020 assets of $16,000 and liabilities of $4,000. It is known that there has been no change to share capital during these two years, and that there was a loss of $550 in FY 2020. What was the profit or loss during FY 2019?

Question 7-1

Identify which two elements increase or decrease due to the following transactions.

i   A company pays immediately for equipment repairs from its bank account.

ii   Interest is paid from a bank account.

iii A patent is bought and will be paid for three months from now.

iv The patent in example iii is paid for.

v   A customer places an order for goods which are not in inventory yet. The customer pays in advance.

vi Amortization of an intangible asset is calculated and input to the accounting records.

vii Insurance is paid for the current month.

viii A corporation tax liability is paid.

Question 7-2

Just after incorporation, a company has the following transactions in its first month, in the order below. All payments or receipts went through the bank account.

A)   Write journals showing the debit and credit entries required.

i   1,000 shares were issued and payment of $10 each was made.

ii   A computer was purchased for $1,500 and paid for immediately.

iii   Inventory was bought for $200 and paid for immediately.

iv   All the inventory was sold on credit for $420.

v   Rent of $ 100 was paid for the current month.

vi   Full payment was received for the sales on credit.

vii   Stationery was bought for $22.

viii Further inventory was bought for $280, this time on credit.

ix A part-time worker was paid $300.

B)   What was the balance on the bank account after the rent was paid, and is it a debit or a credit balance?

C)   What is the balance on the bank account at the end of the month, and is it a debit or a credit balance?

Question 8-1

Company F's workers earn wages and salaries totaling $10,000 in June. F pays its workers during the month they perform the work.

Company G's workers also earn wages and salaries totaling $10,000 in June. G pays its workers in the month after they perform the work.

i   What journal would you expect to see in F's books relating to June wages and salaries?

ii   What journal would you expect to see in G's books relating to June wages and salaries?

iii What other journal created in June would you expect to see in G's books relating to wages and salaries?

iv What would be the difference between F and G's balance sheet every month, based on their timings of wages and salaries payments?

Question 8-2

A company has a fiscal year ending on 31 December 2019. During January 2020, it calculates the tax due on 2019 profits as being $ 11,000. It pays the tax on 26 February 2020. What journals are required and into which fiscal years should they be put?

Question 9-1

An accounting staff member counts a business's cash and finds there is $482. However, the cash account in the ledger shows a debit balance of $480. It is not possible to find what caused the error. What should be done? If an accounting entry is needed, what should it be?

Question 9-2

A A company makes two sales on credit on different days, one to Mr. Smith for $1,200 and one for $2,000 to Company X. Mr. Smith pays in full after two weeks. Company X does not, and eventually information is received that company X has gone bankrupt. Create journals for these transactions, assuming the goods will not be returned by company X.

B Suppose, contrary to expectations, some weeks later, the bankrupt company X does make a final partial payment, of $500. What journal should be written?

Question 10-1

This is the trial balance of a company after it has finished all its accounting entries for the year, except the transfer to retained earnings. Note that the accounts in the trial balance are stated in alphabetical order. What final journal needs to be created?

Trial balance - XYZ Inc.	Dr	Cr
Accounts payable		3,421
Accounts receivable	2,231	
Advertising	2,800	
Bank account	1,801	
Cost of sales	12,420	
Depreciation	400	
Inventories	7,670	
Machinery	1,200	
Prepayments	290	
Rent	7,800	
Retained earnings		10,923
Salaries	2,482	
Sales		26,000
Share capital		2,000
Utilities	3,250	
Totals	42,344	42,344

Question 10-2

An accountant reviews the 21 to 31 May accounts receivable account for errors in a company's ledger. What two things look wrong and why?

Account name : Accounts receivable			Fiscal year : 2019			
Month	**Day**	**Other account**	**Description**	**Dr**	**Cr**	**Balance**
		....	....			38,162
May	21	Sales	DEF Trading - credit sale	1,200		36,962
May	23	Sales	Oak Retail - credit sale	339		36,623
May	23	Bank	Gee Inc - payment		852	37,475
May	25	Sales	Jonas – cash sale	1,000		36,475
May	31	Bank	Electricity April	455		36,020
May	31	Bank	Coral Limited - payment		3,300	39,320

Balance sheet for use with ratio analysis questions 11-1 and 11-2.

Balance sheet

	2017	2018	2019
Current Assets			
Inventories	22,925	23,425	42,412
Accounts receivable	26,329	34,220	38,420
Cash and cash equivalents	3,531	58,540	30,408
Marketable securities	200	190	250
Other current assets	1,145	31	296
Total current assets	54,130	116,406	111,786
Non-Current Assets			
Property, plant & equipment	112,039	115,428	165,324
Intangible Assets	24,674	27,425	26,235
Total non-current assets	136,713	142,853	191,559
Total assets	190,843	259,259	303,345
Current Liabilities			
Accounts payable	27,291	29,824	54,013
Other current liabilities	245	250	7,190
Short-term borrowings	20,800	19,500	18,500
Tax payables	2,345	42,000	34,851
Total current liabilities	50,681	91,574	114,554

Non-current liabilities

Long-term borrowings	135,431	134,300	114,025
Total non-current liabilities	135,431	134,300	114,025
Total liabilities	186,112	225,874	228,579
Equity			
Share Capital	2,000	2,000	12,200
Retained Earnings	2,731	31,385	62,566
Total shareholders' equity	4,731	33,385	74,766
Total liabilities and equity	190,843	259,259	303,345
Sales			
Total sales (assume all on credit)	363,204	383,611	432,915
Cost of sales	168,350	169,216	219,611
Expenses (detail omitted)	192,123	185,741	182,123
Profit after tax	2,731	28,654	31,181
Number of shares	200	200	1,220

Question 11-1

Using the balance sheet information given, calculate the following ratios for the fiscal years indicated, and comment on whether they are getting better or worse, for 2017, 2018 and 2019.

i   current ratio

ii quick ratio

iii debt to equity ratio (using all liabilities)

iv debt to equity ratio (using borrowings only)

v assets to liabilities ratio

Question 11-2

Using the balance sheet and profit and loss account information given, calculate the following ratios for the fiscal years indicated, and comment on whether they are getting better or worse, for 2018 and 2019.

i   Return on assets

ii Return on equity

iii Net profit margin

iv Gross profit margin

v   Operating expenses ratio

vi Earnings per share

vii Inventory turnover ratio

viii Average number of days in inventory

ix Receivables turnover

x   Average collection period

Question 12-1

A business is going to make a decision regarding an outdated machine it owns but no longer uses in its business. Which of these numbers should be used in making the decision?

i   The cost when it was new of the machine.

ii   The current net book value of the machine.

iii The amount that would be received if the machine was disposed of.

iv   Costs relating to disposing of the machine.

v   The profit or loss on disposal that would be recorded if the machine was disposed of.

vi   The amount it would cost to upgrade the machine so it could be usefully used once more in the business.

Question 12-2

Catherine has started a new business, and estimates her fixed costs at $500 per month. She sells a drink which she obtains for $10 a bottle from the makers, and can sell it for $12 a bottle. How many does she need to sell to make a monthly profit of $1,000?

Question 13-1

A company makes its product in two different factories, A and B, which have different cost structures. Given the following facts, what sales price would mean both factories were equally profitable? And what would that profit be?

Factory A: fixed costs 1,000, quantity produced 1,000, variable cost per unit 40

Factory B: fixed costs 5,000, quantity produced 4,000, variable cost per unit 51

Question 13-2

Company A and Company B sell a similar product at the same price. Company A has fixed costs of $200 and variable costs of $20 per unit. Company B has fixed costs of $400 and variable costs of $16. What is the quantity and unit sales price at which these companies will have the same break-even point?

Index

日本語事項索引

＜著者紹介＞

スチュアート・ブライソン（Stuart Brison）

英国公認会計士（Chartered Accountant）

横浜国立大学非常勤講師・横浜市立大学非常勤講師

1960年生まれ。1982年，Heriot Watt University, Department of Actuarial Mathematics and Statistics卒業，1988年公認会計士の資格取得。Touche Ross & Co.（現デロイト・トウシュ・トーマツ），スイス銀証券会社，ABN AMRO証券会社を経て，公認会計士事務所開業。

＜主要業績＞

『アカウンティング (MBAエッセンシャル講座)』共著，中央経済社，2003年

＜訳者紹介＞

原　俊雄（はら　としお）　　担当：第1章－第3章，第7章－第11章

横浜国立大学大学院国際社会科学研究院教授

1966年生まれ。1989年横浜国立大学経営学部卒業，1991年横浜国立大学大学院経営学研究科修士課程修了，1994年一橋大学大学院商学研究科博士後期課程単位修得退学。文教大学情報学部講師，助教授，横浜国立大学経営学部助教授，教授を経て2013年より現職。会計検査院特別研究官（2004-2006年），カーディフ大学客員研究員（2011-2012年），2020-2022年度税理士試験委員。

＜主要業績＞

『簿記と帳簿組織の機能－歴史的・国際的視点から』編著，中央経済社，2019年

『簿記テキスト（第6版）』共著，中央経済社，2022年

『テキスト会計学講義（第2版）』編著，中央経済社，2022年

大森　明（おおもり　あきら）　　担当：第4章－第6章，第12章，第13章

横浜国立大学大学院国際社会科学研究院教授

1971年生まれ。1994年青山学院大学経営学部第二部卒業，1996年横浜国立大学大学院経営学研究科修士課程修了，2000年同大学大学院国際開発研究科博士課程後期修了，博士（学術）。愛知学院大学商学部講師，助教授，横浜国立大学経営学部准教授を経て現職。会計検査院特別研究官（2010-2012年），マッコーリ大学客員研究員（2014-2015年），第4次尾瀬総合学術調査団基礎研究部会調査員（2017-2020年）を歴任。

＜主要業績＞

『マクロ会計入門―国民経済計算への会計的アプローチ』共著，中央経済社，2012年

『テキスト会計学講義（第2版）』分担執筆，中央経済社，2022年

"Drivers of Corporate Water Related Disclosure: Evidence from Japan", 共著, *Journal of Cleaner Production*, Vol. 129, 2016

英語で学ぶ会計入門

2020年5月1日　第1版第1刷発行
2023年9月25日　第1版第4刷発行

著　者　スチュアート・ブライソン
訳　者　原　　　俊　雄
　　　　大　森　　　明
発行者　山　本　　　継
発行所　㈱中 央 経 済 社
発売元　㈱中央経済グループ
　　　　パブリッシング
〒101-0051　東京都千代田区神田神保町1-35
電　話　03 (3293) 3371 (編集代表)
　　　　03 (3293) 3381 (営業代表)
https://www.chuokeizai.co.jp
印刷／三英グラフィック・アーツ㈱
製本／誠　製　本　㈱

© 2020
Printed in Japan